Renaissance WOMAN

A Feminine Midlife Crisis

FROM LOSS OF IDENTITY TO REBIRTH

FABIENNE SLAMA

1st edition, I, MMXV

Author: Fabienne Slama
Title: Renaissance Woman
ISBN: 978-1-77204-028-9
Category: BODY, MIND & SPIRIT/Healing/General

Publisher:
Black Card Books™
Division of Gerry Robert Enterprises Inc.
Suite 214, 5-18 Ringwood Drive
Stouffville, Ontario
Canada, L4A 0N2
International Calling: 1-647-361-8577
www.blackcardbooks.com

Printed in the United States of America

Renaissance WOMAN

A Feminine Midlife Crisis

FROM LOSS OF IDENTITY TO REBIRTH

FABIENNE SLAMA

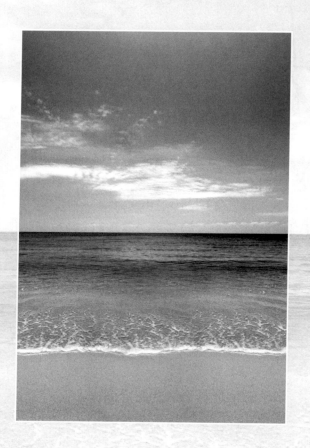

TABLE OF CONTENTS

FOREWORD

Renaissance Woman

I am a beautiful sandy beach caressed
by smooth waves rolling back and forth.

I am the sound of children playing in the sand.
I am their fun. I am their joy of being together
under the open sky.

I am a ripe piece of pineapple going down my throat.
I am sweet and tangy at the same time.
I am this beautiful fruity flavor.

I am the salt in the water.
I am the heat on the shore: quiet and deep.

I am the sand rolling under my feet: warm and soft.

I am at peace. I am peace. I am.

- Fabienne Slama

According to the *American Heritage Dictionary*, "Renaissance" is described as the cultural rebirth that occurred in Europe between the fourteenth century through the middle of the seventeenth century based on the rediscovery of Greece and Rome. During the Renaissance, America was discovered and the Reformation began. Modern times are often considered to have begun with the Renaissance. It was a great period of revival in the world of art, sciences, spirituality, and learning in general, a time when individual potentiality prevailed over a more contemplative life.

More generally, Renaissance means "rebirth" or "reawakening," and it is what many ordinary women like you and me in our modern society will experience at one point or another in our lives.

I am one of those Renaissance women. A few years ago, I transformed myself inside out and observed my own rebirth. As an artist, I have always represented strong and sensuous ladies out of clay and bronze. Today, I acknowledge that I am a woman as beautiful as my creations. As a scientist and a spiritual being, I wish to help others. Today, I am proud to be a therapist working with the tools of emotional healing therapy, core energy coaching, and hypnosis to guide hundreds of friends, women, and men through their own transition from professional to personal change, depression, and anger management. I hope to achieve a next level through this book by enabling my readers to acquire the basic tools to help themselves.

This book is about discovering your own path toward rebirth. The examples I use are not only based on my own journey, but also on the challenges my clients have faced. Obviously, for confidentiality reason, names have been modified. On your self-rediscovery path, you will to have face your fears, but once you decide to move forward, you will find a beautiful woman, a strong woman, a woman you can love unconditionally—a Renaissance woman. You will find YOU.

This book is dedicated to my mom, Mona, and all the strong women in my family. You are my inspiration.

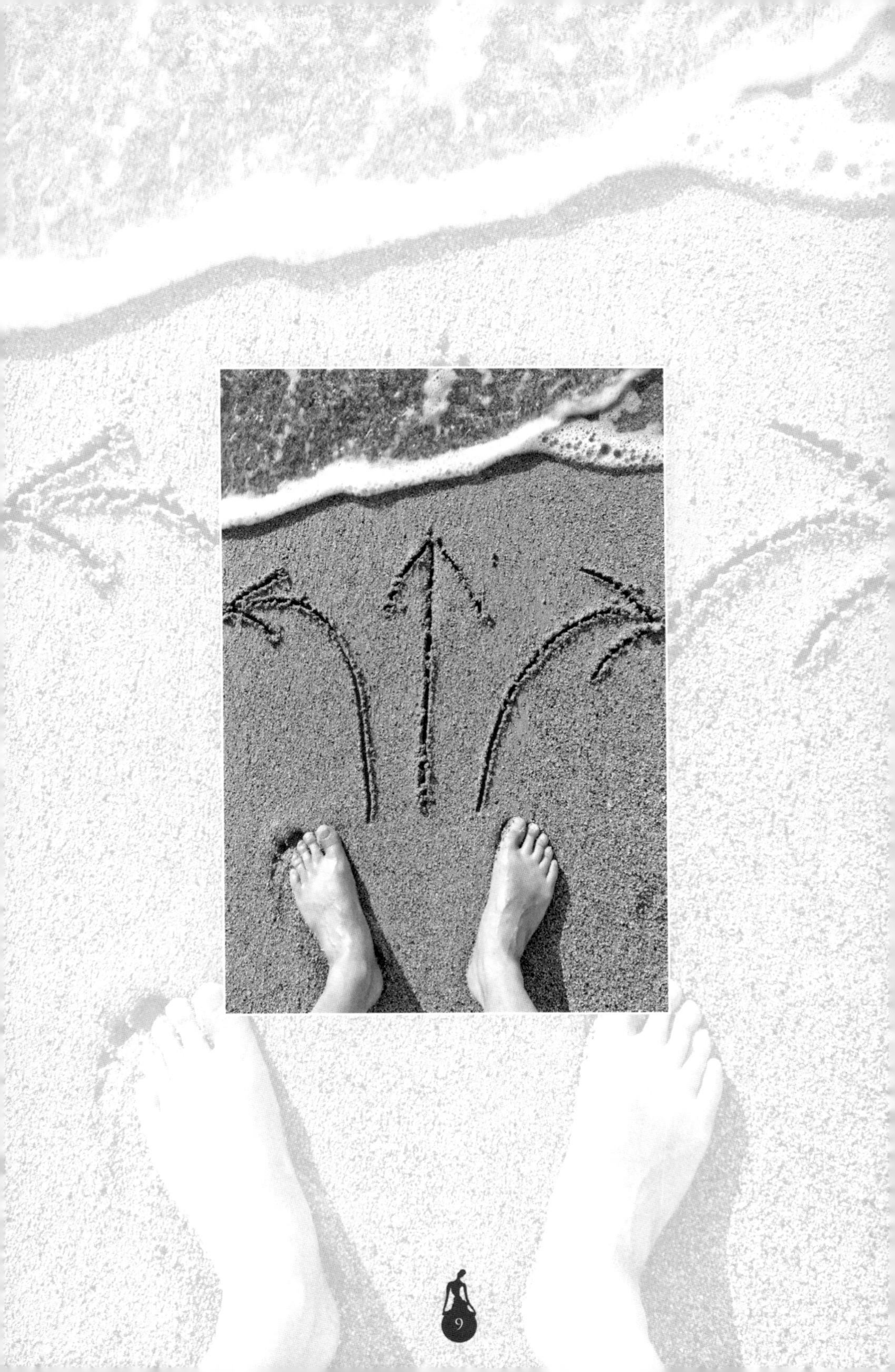

INTRODUCTION

A World of Tens

*"And the day came
when the risk to remain tight in a bud
was more painful than the risk it took to blossom."*

- Anais Nin

I was born in 1968, which makes me forty-six at the time of this writing, the perfect age for coming out of what many would call a "midlife crisis." In the past few years, I changed my story from *I am not lovable* to one that says *I love myself.* I chose to recognize my own value and became proud of who I am. I decided to be grateful to be alive and to smile each time I have the opportunity. I am proud to announce that I am a Renaissance woman.

I have been unhappy in a perfectly good life for way too many years. I cried about what I was not. I lingered on a past that was not what I had hoped for, and I fussed over the fact that I was not living up to my own expectation. I moaned over my present and worried about a future that wasn't in my control. I had everything to be happy, yet I was still miserable. I had absolutely no excuse to feel that way. I was blessed with an easy childhood, loving parents, a great husband, and wonderful children. I had almost everything, but I was not able to appreciate it for one simple thing was missing in my life: ME. I had forgotten who I was.

As I entered my forties, I started feeling lost. I judged myself as unworthy and forgot how it felt to simply smile. I didn't like myself anymore. I fell into depression and lay on the ground crying over my own story, the one I didn't realize I had chosen. I believed that voice in my head that kept repeating over and over, "You're not good enough. You are not living up to your full potential. You are a spouse, a mom, a daughter, a friend, but you are not enough. You are not you. Do even know who you are? And, more importantly, even if you knew who you were, are you the person you really want to be? Are you proud of yourself? Are you living the life that you are meant to live? Are you at peace with yourself?"

Like you, I had a childhood dream, a simple dream. Like yours, my dream included a sense of happiness, fulfillment, and overall bliss. What was your dream? A great family? A purposeful career? Enough money to travel around the world? Becoming famous? What happened to that dream? What happened to you? When did you stop trying and became a middle-aged woman struggling with doubts?

Does this sound familiar? For the longest time, I thought I was the only one. However, when I shared this feeling with other women, I discovered that so many of us are living this type of story day after day—an average story for an average midlife woman.

Who are we? We are usually the forty- and fifty-year-olds who spent the past twenty to thirty years of our lives defined in relation to others. We moved along this path called "life." We were kids who became teenagers and young adults with dreams we fulfilled or not. We flew from our twenties to our thirties and straight into our forties. We got married or not. We started a family or not. We chose a career unless one was imposed on us for financial reasons or because it was expected from us. We put one foot in front of the other and advanced in life without questioning it. We lost our consciousness into action. We had our good times and hurtful ones. We had to compromise on our ambitions and make choices that we didn't necessarily want to make.

Then suddenly, as if for no reason, something or someone made us stop, and when we looked around, we realized we didn't know who we were anymore. We paused and didn't recognize our dream life. We realized that we got off the path we wanted. We reached the point where we say, "Enough is enough. I want to be me. I have the right to be me." But before we can be ourselves, we need to answer this simple question: *Who am I*? We would like to believe in ourselves, but are we good enough? Are we worth loving ourselves after so many years?

To answer this question, let's try a little game. Imagine that I offer you a one-hundred dollar bill. It's straight from the bank, fresh and crisp, and smells of fresh money. How much is it worth? One hundred dollars, right?

Now, let's imagine that I fold the bill in half and then again in half. It's still worth one hundred dollars, right? Now, I crinkle the bill into a ball and toss it on the ground into the mud. Then I step on it, pick it up, and tear it a little in the corners without destroying it but damaging it nonetheless. Now what is its value? It's still one hundred dollars. Are you sure? Of course you are. No matter how damaged the bill, it still keeps the same value.

Life damages us. We get hurt, our feeling get bruised, we get older...A bill will not lose its value regardless of how it was treated. Still, we believe that life events lessen our self-value over time. Are we less worthy because life had some impact on us? I don't think so anymore, but I did for the longest time. So many women think less of themselves because something or someone told them they were not loveable or because they told themselves so.

We have to remember that we are born whole, perfect, and complete. We come into this world as perfect as possible, with our absolute best potential living inside of us. We are "ten out of ten." I was a ten, and so were you. What happens to a baby girl who was a ten for her to become an adult woman and feel that she is not enough? It's simple: life happens, judgment happens. From day one, we create our own life story, our own paradigm based on many parameters: our family history, our gender, our race, our experiences at home, and at school. And from day one, this influences our experience of what life is about.

Paradigm is a typical example or pattern of something; a pattern or model (Oxford English dictionary).

Our paradigm is the way we experience life according to our own life experience, our story.

As soon as we gain consciousness, we compare ourselves to those who surround us. By doing so, we start judging ourselves. "Look at Mary, her hair is nicer than mine. Look at John, he runs faster than me. Alicia is better at math, and Brian's drawings are nicer than mine." And so on. Through this process, our self-grade changes. We, little tens, start considering ourselves as less. We give ourselves our own "lower grade" and we become sevens, sixes, or twos depending on how we feel about who we are. We don't see that Brian may be gifted with wonderful drawing skills but his running abilities are not the best. We try to be perfect at everything, and since perfection in everything isn't achievable, we start considering ourselves as defective. This process starts at birth and goes on for the rest of our lives, and after some point, we just forget how much potential we have.

At a young age, our self-evaluation process depends on how the people we admire and respect the most make us feel and what they tell us about who we are. Those people are our parents, our family members, our teachers, any authority figure, and later on in life, our peers. You are lucky if your parents remind you that you are still a ten—whole, perfect, and complete—because you will start with a sense of self-worth that others may lack. Our parents—the way they respond to life, and the way they behave with us—will impact the way we see life. If they teach us peace, self-worth, respect, and love, we will grow more confident. If they teach us fear, doubt, and pain, we will be probably more afraid of new experiences. As early as four or five years old, we develop a good sense of what is safe or not safe, of what feels good or dangerous. We are still innocent, and we are not yet armed to shape our own opinion on the way things are supposed to be. We tend to react at a very primal level, and unfortunately what is learned during those early times can impact us for years and sometimes for the rest of our life unless our paradigm is challenged.

We are all born whole, perfect, and complete. We just forgot.

I will use an example of one of my clients to explain how insidious and long lasting the effects of childhood's experience can be.

Little Chloe was born with an alcoholic father who would come back home after drinking and behave violently. Chloe had two younger siblings, and her mom was so depressed that she barely got out of bed. When Chloe got home from school, she had two options: she could go out and play with other kids her age, or she could clean up the house, take care of her siblings, and make sure everything looked as tidy as possible before her father

came home. The few times she chose to play, her father had become very angry and punished her. She quickly learned that having fun was dangerous.

Today, as a wonderful, smart, fifty-year-old, Chloe has four kids of her own and is married to a wonderful, loving man, but she is exhausted. She goes to work, comes home, takes care of her house, then takes care of her family. She never stops. She never relaxes. She never takes time for herself. She wants to take time for herself, and her family encourages it, but each times she goes out even for a walk or to get a manicure, she feels so tense that she doesn't enjoy it. She usually cuts it short only to come back home for more chores. Why is that? It's not because Chloe doesn't want to enjoy life; she wishes she could. But little five-year-old Chloe is the one who is in control of adult Chloe's emotions. The lessons she had learned so early in life taught her that having fun or relaxing was dangerous. Those lessons don't serve her anymore. Her father had passed away a long time ago, and she is a grown woman. Still, the five-year-old Chloe, who served her so well to be safe as a little girl, became the master of her life, preventing adult Chloe from enjoying her present.

It seems so strange, even ridiculous, but more often than not, our perception of life comes from our early childhood and it is difficult to stray from this. Our brain might tell us that we are safe, but still it is very difficult to change, and we move along without questioning why certain things trigger stress in us.

As we grow older, the impact of our parents' teaching might lessen, but the influence from our partner, friends, coworkers, or even the media will increase. Lessons will be learned from different experiences in life, and we will go from one cycle of change to another.

I have spent the past fifteen years sculpting women. Each time I take a pack of clay and place it in front of me, I realize it has all the potential to become a masterpiece. I take my tools, cut here, shape there, enhance this feature, and erase one line or another. But whatever shape it takes, this piece of art will still have the same potential, the same value it had when it was just raw clay, and as long as the clay stays soft and malleable, it can be reshaped again and again.

Life acts on women exactly the same way as those tools. Every little girl is born with the potential of becoming someone amazing. She will evolve differently depending on the environment, her surroundings, the people she will meet along her life, and her circumstances. As a girl in a twenty-first century society, a lot will be expected from her, and fortunately, most girls can become almost anything they want in this day and age. It's a wonderful progress but also creates a lot of pressure. Young ladies of today have to be so many things: pretty, smart, athletic, socially integrated, creative, etc. They have to live up to so many expectations. As they enter adulthood, they will have to reshape themselves over and over again according to external or internal requirements. Whatever their journey looks like, they will go from one change to another, sometimes having to face more than simply a change. They will have to confront a transition.

CHAPTER 1

The Cycle of Change

"Who are you?", said the Caterpillar.
"I – I hardly know sir, just at present—at least I know who I was when I got up this morning, but I think I must have changed several times since then."

- Alice's Adventures in Wonderland by Lewis Carroll

I entered my forties wondering who I was. I had started to slowly but surely remove myself from the social world. I pretended to work on promoting my art, but I was in fact spending four to five hours a day sitting on the sofa watching TV. I had gained over thirty pounds in few months and was feeling terrible about my body. I was missing my family. My parents were in Europe, my oldest son was in college, and I knew my second son would follow in a couple of years. The relationship with my husband was not at its best, and I wasn't sure we would stay together once we became "empty nesters."

At the same time, I realized we had a good life. Not great, but good enough. We were healthy, wealthy enough, our kids were good kids, and we were living in beautiful California in a nice home. What was I complaining about? Maybe I was spoiled by life and didn't have big-enough concerns to make me realize that my life was exactly what it was supposed to be. Happiness doesn't come from the outside; it is something you find inside of you, and I had lost my *joie de vivre*.

This "good life" ended when one of my fears became reality: my husband decided to leave me. I had become single after being married for twenty years. I went into deep depression and seriously considered hurting myself. One night, I contemplated swallowing forty painkillers I had found in my house to stop the emotional pain. Just before acting on it, I remember asking the universe to send me a message one last time. I closed my eyes to reflect on what I was about to do and the universe responded to my request in a beautiful way. I slept for seven hours straight.

After three weeks of sleepless nights disturbed by panic attacks, this was a blessing. I woke up the next day and realized that I was emotionally exhausted but I was not ready to end it here. I started reconnecting with the world and reached out for help. Well-intentioned people told me I would see the light at the end of the tunnel, but at the time I couldn't even find the entrance to that tunnel. Finding Randy, a coach and hypnotherapist, to help me through this challenging phase was a blessing. Within six weeks, I was convinced that I would live again. After nine weeks of intense self-work, I was back on my feet going to my first party as a single woman. Merely two months after my husband left, I started my own training as a transition coach so I could help others the way I had been with regression hypnosis, emotional healing therapy, NLP (Neuro-Linguistic Programming), and coaching.

Within a year, I sold my house, found a smaller one, and started a new life, one where I am now thriving. I assume myself financially for the first time. I am surrounded by friends and people I love. I have met mentors, teachers, friends, and fascinating people in general. I have developed a great coaching practice and have wonderful clients. I am writing this book and fulfilling my childhood dream of helping others, one person at a time, while continuing to work on that second passion of mine—sculpture.

I had to face many personal changes along my life, good ones and more challenging ones:

- Changing school every year from kindergarten to senior year.
- Moving to a different country, changing careers multiple times (I was a biochemist, a teacher, a journalist, a PR person, an artist, and a mom).
- Recovering from a bad back injury.
- Getting married.
- Having kids.
- Seeing my oldest son go to college across the country.
- Hearing my husband say that he didn't love me anymore.

Each of these events impacted me tremendously. But somehow, this last challenge in my forties triggered something different. I went through a real transition, something that was more than a simple change.

The difference between a change and what I would call a "transition" is subtle; the impact of change will be short-lived while a transition can last a lifetime. Change is situational. We move, we grow up, our family situation evolves, all of which creates change in a person. Sometimes, those changes trigger something bigger in our psyche, but we don't always need a real trigger to experience an emotional transformation or transition. Through life—through nature in general—things can go slowly for a time when nothing seems

> **Change** is situational and its impact on the psyche is usually short-lived.
>
> **Transition** is an emotional transformation. It can be triggered by a change, but sometimes it seems to just happen. Its effect will last a lifetime.

to happen until a sudden acceleration and a deep transformation occurs. Inner reorientation and self-redefinition are what defines a transition. To continue with the sculpture metaphor, if change feels like reshaping the clay, transition looks more like pounding on the soft clay to bring it back to its original form and starting a piece anew. Transition can be brutal, challenging, and scary, but it's often the only way to go back to this possibility of creating a masterpiece. In sculpting, you have to destroy the original shape, find a new concept, and model a brand-new piece.

My own transition affected the way I saw the world surrounding me, but most importantly, the way I viewed myself. Not because it was dramatic, not because my family life changed drastically, not because I added another career to the many ones I already had. I didn't change for any external reason. I changed because I finally decided to be me and to exist according to my own principle and values.

This is the happy ending to my story, but the first steps on that journey seemed hazardous since every transition has to begin with an end. It was the end of who I thought I was, and I wasn't certain I was ready to let go of the old me. It was terrifying. I was feeling miserable, ugly, tired, undervalued, and not lovable, but at least I knew those feelings. They were familiar, and familiar feels comfortably safer than the unknown. I had to let go of my own not-so-flattering self-image, and I didn't know who I would find once I removed that mask. I had to jump and I was scared. Fortunately, at that point, I didn't have much to lose anymore. I jumped and discovered that letting go of yourself can be painful, but it is only as painful as you let it to be. At the same time, you feel a thrilling experience when you let go of the fear.

Every transition has to begin with the end.

I had the opportunity to work with many women in the past years. Even though each had their own story, the message they shared was very similar. Whether they were married or single, with or without children, whatever was their profession, each of them contacted me with similar concerns: ***I have an okay life, but I don't think I live up to my full potential. I think I might be depressed or overwhelmed. I don't know who I am anymore. I am always defined by my role with others, but I am tired of that. I don't live the life I would like. I don't enjoy my work anymore. I want to follow my passion, which doesn't mean that I want to get a divorce or quit my job; it just means that I want to be me.***

Wanting a fulfilling life might be considered a luxury problem observed mostly in our wealthy society. It is true that when you don't know how you're going to feed yourself or your family tomorrow, you may not have the time to reflect on who you are. However, this problem is far from being meaningless. Women going through midlife crises are hurting. They feel they've lost their identity, and having something that society would qualify as "a good enough reason" doesn't make it easier. If anything, it makes most of them wonder why they feel that way and feel guilty as well as feeling lost. So, if you have been feeling this way, just know that you are not the only one. Most women between the age of forty and sixty will reach this transition point at one time or another, and many men will face a crisis of their own.

When good enough is not good enough anymore, you have a choice to make: sit and cry, or understand it's time to change something.

Men versus Women Quest for Identity

This book will mostly focus on the feminine version of what scientists call "midlife crisis," but this is far from being a woman-only issue. For the longest time, a midlife crisis has been a man stereotype. The pattern described for the masculine version is more likely to be caused by work issues and usually lasts longer than for their female counterpart (three to ten years versus two to five years[1]).

1 Diller, Vivian. *Face It: What Women Really Feel as Their Looks Change.* Hay House, 2010

The man will recognize that he is not getting any younger, that he has been focusing a lot of his energy on his career, that he has been a provider for the family with many responsibilities weighing on his shoulders. He is reaching a point in life when he wants to enjoy life and reconnect with his younger self with dreams and aspirations. He might feel the pressure of being professionally and financially "successful" before reaching retirement age. The American stereotype is that men tend to buy themselves expensive "toys": a sports car, a motorcycle, or any exciting object they've always desired. They also consider their relationship less exciting and less fulfilling, looking outside to get reassured about their role as an individual. Usually, it is at this stage that many men get into an extramarital affair. I conversed with many men in their fifties and heard the same statements about their professional dissatisfaction: "This is my last chance at work, so I better make it." On the relationship level, the struggle was mostly about being underappreciated: "I did what was expected from me, but I had become part of the furniture. She doesn't recognize my value and I want to be seen."

Few men go for the younger-prettier-sexier stereotype but not all, and it is understandable that the path from feeling undervalued to getting into an affair is a very short one. Is the cliché of "sports car, young girl" still part of men's midlife crisis? It is only part of the story, but it is certainly a reality.

The trigger of a female midlife crisis seems to be mostly due to a personal evaluation of her role. Women experience midlife crises nowadays differently than in the past. Women reaching their forties used to be transitioning from being mothers to being free of kids. Today, women have a spot in the workplace and have high expectations for themselves, which often reaches a point to when fulfillment is no longer about financial or hierarchy success but more about proving their value by making a significant difference in the world. Some of those women quit their regular job altogether in the hope of self-discovery. If they never focused on their career, they might decide to join the workforce to make up for lost time. As a matter of fact, women are facing a midlife quest for identity more than a crisis per se. They crave to realize their potential and achieve their goal.

The smart, goal-driven, highly educated women are not really looking to recover their youth but are instead searching to uncover their "greatness," whatever this word means to them. Unfulfilled and disoriented, they will have to challenge themselves to discover what reaching their goal looks like to them.

The Cycle of Change

There is not one midlife crisis, since each individual is different. We each have our own life story, our own paradigm, and our own way of reacting to stress. Nevertheless, we can describe the four most common phases in the cycle of change or transition:

- The end or letting go.
- The limbo.
- The rebirth.
- Playing your hand.

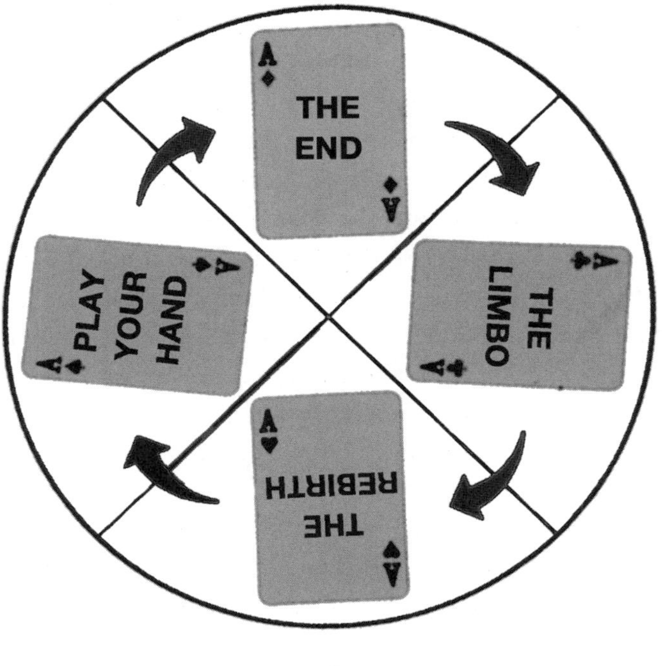

You have to accept that in order to have a new beginning—a rebirth—the first step is unfortunately the end: letting go. We must learn how to let go of our old truth, our paradigm, our belief, our "good enough," and sometimes even our values, while also letting go of our own limitations, our blocks, and our fears. The second step, or limbo, is no less challenging. Because we had to let go of so many references of the past, we reach this existential question: *Who am I?* Then comes the fun part of creating your own future and enjoying the new you.

Part of redefining who you are is to separate what you like about yourself and want to keep from what you would like or have to let go of. A few years ago, my self-definition would have been, "I am a spouse, a mom, a good friend, and an artist who is expressing herself mostly through her sculptures." When this transition hit me, I had no choice but to let go of the "spouse" part of me. I can assure you that it was extremely strange; after twenty years of wearing the "spouse" hat, I had to return to the "single woman" status. My kids were growing up and, even though I was still their mom and will be for the rest of my life, my role as a mother had evolved to be more of a friend to my teenage and young adult children.

I kept what I enjoyed in my life. I still consider myself a good friend, but I developed new friendships with people I would not have connected to before. I was not particularly looking for different people, but I had become so foreign to who I was that I attracted individuals I would have never connected with before. Today, I am open to new relationships and new friendships. I am way less judgmental of others' choices in life since I finally understand that life is not a linear journey but more a series of crossings. I am still an artist and I've developed a few other means of expression beyond sculpting: dancing, writing, playing, and professionally coaching people who are looking for my support.

I have added one more adornment to this definition of who I am: I am a woman. In the past years, I had forgotten the essential of my essence to become mom and wife. I realize that I am a woman and proud to be one. That implies that I have the sensitivity of a woman, the femininity of a woman, and the strength of a woman. During my limbo, I searched for the type of woman I wanted to be, and during my rebirth, I became that beautiful woman according to my own definition: feminine, strong, smart, vulnerable, and unstoppable.

Once I managed to rediscover myself, I moved out from this transition phase and started living my life. The process could be compared to an onion. I went through this journey layer after layer, each time letting go of the past and of my old paradigm, each time finding myself lost not knowing what was my truth anymore, and fortunately, each time finding my new truth and establishing the new rules I wanted to live by. Each step was challenging and each step was fascinating. I considered many times numbing the pain with antidepressants, but it would have actually been just that: "numbing the pain," and in consequence, delaying the work that I needed to do. As difficult as it was, pain was part of the process. I understand that sometimes it gets unbearable, but I made the choice to go through that without medication.

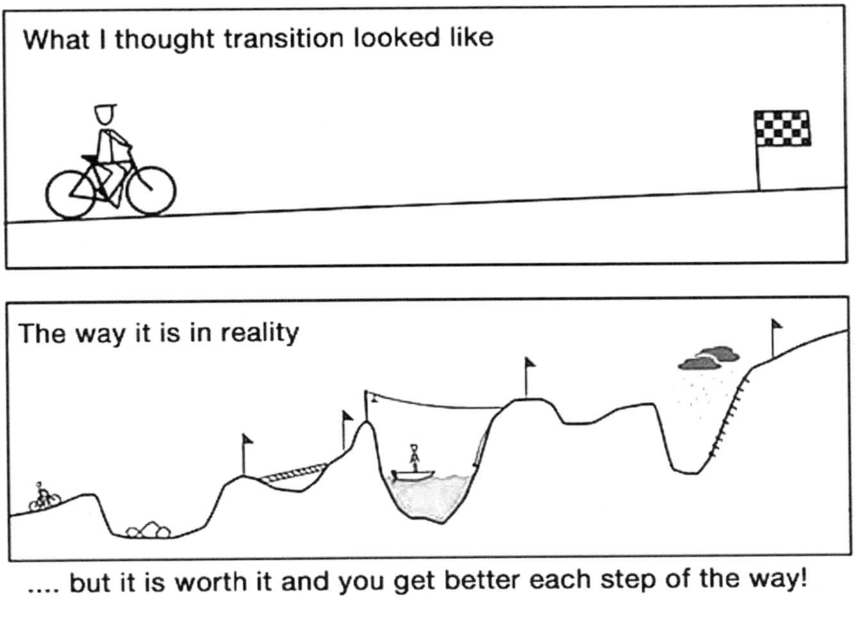

What I thought transition looked like
The way it is in reality

.... but it is worth it and you get better each step of the way!

I was not in a pathologic chronic depression. I was displaying symptoms of depression and anxiety because I was going through a difficult time. I'm not saying that you have to make the same choices I made. You have to make the best choice for you. Mine was to not take medication, and I don't regret it. It was painful and terrible at times. I had panic attacks, and I woke up many nights drench in cold sweat when I was lucky enough to catch some sleep. My stomach shut itself up and I lost fifteen pounds in less than three weeks. I thought about killing myself many times, but I emerged quicker from this process than a lot of people. I know many who chose the chemical path, whether it is prescribed drugs, non-prescribed drugs, alcohol, or any other way people use to quiet their feelings. I learned from that experience that I could go through many predicaments and emerge stronger on the other side.

Reaching for Help

I didn't go through the whole process on my own. If there is one thing I would like you to remember from this book, it is DON'T GO THROUGH IT ALONE—REACH FOR HELP. Part of making it on your own is to know to ask for support when you need it. Be very specific about the type of help you want.

I first went to a classically trained psychologist, but that was not the right person for me. She asked me to tell my story and to stay strong. After a two-hour session, I said good-bye. This is hard work and you need a great partner in this journey. She was not the right one for me. I was blessed to meet a wonderful coach who later on became my mentor. His favorite saying still lingers with me now: "Every emotion is short-lived unless resisted to."

We too often try to hide from our emotions by ignoring them. We swallow our sadness and anger and focus on work, going out, and keeping busy any way we can. We drink ourselves into oblivion and swallow legal or illegal drugs to take the edge away. We stand strong and pretend to be okay, but ignoring the pain can be extremely detrimental and make us sick in the long term. True courage and actual recovery is often found in addressing the problem instead of running from it. Yes, you might cry, scream, and feel terrible about what is going on in your life, but once you accept that you are just going through natural emotions, the pain associated fades away faster than you can believe. If you need to be sad, just be sad, and if you feel the need to cry, listen to what your body is telling you. If you are angry, take a pillow and pound on it. Keeping the emotions inside is the worst thing you can do to your body.

One of my clients was describing his anger as a punch in the stomach. Every time he thought about his wife leaving him, he felt this punch-in-the-gut sensation. Unfortunately, he wanted to be angry because he believed that letting go of his anger would be a proof of weakness. We had to stop our work when he was diagnosed with stomach cancer. Please let your emotions flow before they poison your body. The pain won't last, and I will explain later in this book how to let the emotional energy move away faster.

> Every emotion is short-lived unless resisted to.

I went through the sadness, anger, guilt, fear, and so many emotions associated with midlife crisis, and yes, it was challenging. Yes, it was scary. Yes, I was lost and miserable. Yes, the divorce didn't help. And yes, I thought I would never recover from it and the only way to make the pain go away would be to stop breathing. Not only did I survive, I actually did way more than that. I found this tunnel my friends were telling me about, entered it, walked through its ups and downs to finally emerge on the other side a better and stronger person.

Women are often blessed with a good network of friends and allies to help in this quest. Ask for their support, for they can be a great way to get some feedback. You might even find that a lot of your friends are facing a similar challenge and asking themselves the same questions. As you listen to your friends' advice, don't let anyone tell you that you have no right to dream your best life. A friend might come in the discussion with his or her own dreams, expectations, or limitations. Don't be stopped by someone else's fears. Don't let anyone tell you that you have no right to be unhappy with your present life and demand something better. This is a challenging time. Searching for your life's purpose can be a daunting experience. Facing questions such as, "What should I have accomplished by this time in my life that I haven't done?" "Is there something more fulfilling that I would like to focus on?" "What do I want in my life for the next year, ten years, forty years, sixty years?" "Am I happy with what I have right now?" "What should I keep or leave?" Obviously, a good coach can be the best source for guidance during this phase.

All the questions above are very significant. It's natural to lose your balance and your sense of purpose when they become part of your journey. You might be at the very beginning of the process, hearing this voice in your head saying you would like more from life. You might be lost in your own life wondering who the person is who looks back at you in the mirror morning after morning. You've lost your identity and you feel that you've lost your emotional compass. Still, you are brave enough to admit, "I don't know who I am." It takes courage to accept that you are not living the life you would like to live. It's actually better to seek for answers than to live a numb existence.

One of the major steps in going through this tunnel will be to admit that it is just a part of a traditional journey toward finding yourself. I've seen it called a "midlife crisis" or a "midlife transition." I've also seen it called a "heroine's journey," because it takes a strong woman to go through this metamorphosis gracefully and emerge from it a better self. Women who are fierce enough to face this overwhelming path, I call "Renaissance women," because once they emerge from it, they are different from who they were when they took their first step. They come out stronger, more creative, open to different possibilities, curious, and they can accomplish so much more than what they initially expected. Let's start on this journey together. It's time to rediscover this wonderful woman, this Renaissance woman, in you.

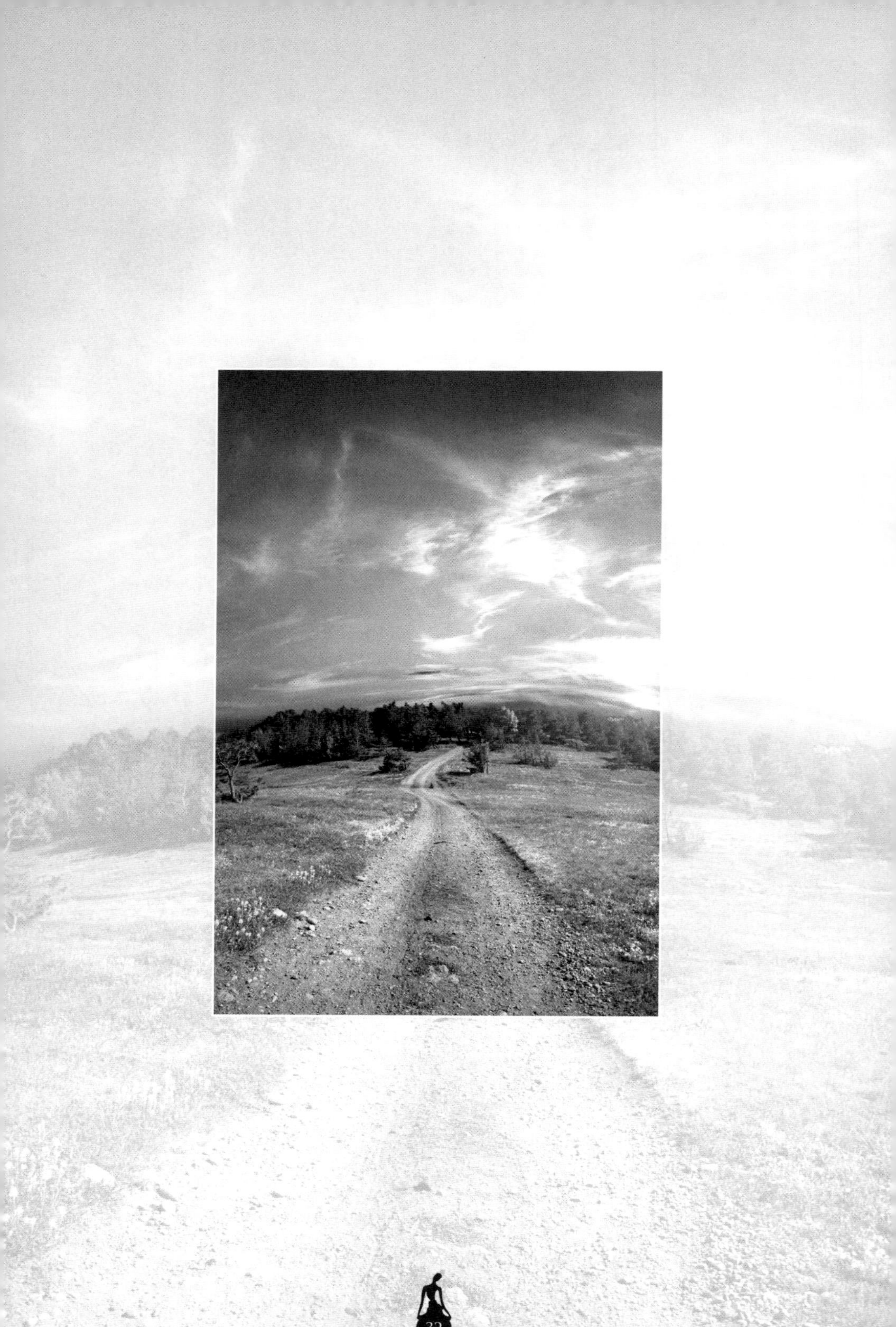

CHAPTER 2

The End-Letting Go of the Past

"In order to know the light, we must first experience the darkness."

- *Carl Jung*

We grow up with plans and aspirations, but we tend to settle for less as we get in touch with our limitations and priorities. It's important to have high standards, and a lot can be achieved with determination, grit, and effort. Sometimes we don't carry out those childhood dreams and our sense of disappointment and failure swallows us. Before starting on this rebirth journey, it is important to realize what success looks like to us. The media constantly shows us those who have reached remarkable success, but the success of the famous might not be one we really want. Embracing a joyful, fulfilling, loving life can achieve success on its own. Sometimes financial success is essential, but it is perfectly fine to focus on love and family instead. The first step to determine what you want is to rate what you are experiencing in your present life.

Rating Your Life

Let's look at a time when you felt happy or neutral about your life, and let's rate it as being your starting point of zero. Here are a few statements I will ask you to consider. For each stressful situation, you will add points, and each time there is an obvious solution, you can subtract some of those points. The number of points added or subtracted will depend on how stressful the situation feels to you. Don't try to be precise; this is just a way to rate what is triggering negative emotions in your life.

These situations are presented in a casual way but are actually representing tangible issues experienced by many women in their midlife.

1. **Your husband wants a new sports car while you would prefer to go on a trip as a family before your kids go to college.**

   Add 100 potential divorce points.

   This is going back to the sports car cliché, but what is shown here is when spouses start wanting different things in life and are not willing to compromise so much anymore, which creates tension and resentment in the couple.

2. **At least one of your parents is old enough that you are constantly concerned about his or her health, or they passed away and you are the oldest one in your generation.**

   Add 400 stress points.

This is the very stressful realization that you are not getting any younger and that the time you have in front of you to realize your dream is limited. There might be stress added by the responsibility of taking care of an elderly parent while still taking care of your children.

3. **You aren't happy about your job and would like to go back to college to get a degree.**

   Add 100 to 300 life purpose points.

   This implies few elements that you may want to look at individually. First, you are not happy about your professional life. Second, you consider the limited amount of time you have in front of you to catch up with your dream. Last but not least, going back to school is expensive, especially at a time when you are considering sending your own kids to college. All those facets can add up to an extremely stressful situation.

4. **You had an affair or are considering having one. You don't communicate anymore with your partner and don't feel appreciated, or your physical intimacy is not what it used to be.**

   Add 200 to 500 stress or potential divorce points.

   You are not satisfied by your relationship. You start doubting the possibility of it lasting. You are starting to look outside of your partner for comfort. One of my friends described it really well. Her kids called her Mom, and her husband called her Mom. She was no longer being viewed as a woman anymore, and she ended up having an affair with someone who was recognizing her for who she was—a beautiful woman. This was a huge step for her, because she had to face the fact that what she wanted the most in a relationship was nowhere to be found anymore with her spouse, and she had to go against some of her values about the importance of keeping a family together. She left a twenty-two-year marriage and designed her new life as an independent woman.

5. **You returned from your high school reunion and realize that others have a better life than you.**

   Add 200 stress points.

   You are starting to compare yourself to others and start challenging what you have. Life doesn't feel good enough anymore. You might consider that you should have done more differently and that you don't have a lot of time left to catch up with your old friends.

   We always compare ourselves to others. Doing so, we start jugging ourselves, and we start considering our value in comparison to what we see in others. It might be true or not, that is not the problem. Each time we are considering ourselves "less than," we lose a part of our self-love.

6. **You are noticing new wrinkles. You consider a face-lift.**

   Add 200 stress points.

   It's true that we get inevitably older, but those signs are starting to bother you. Even though some women take pride in the fact that they look good for their age, they have to accept those changes as a sign that they are getting wiser and wittier. Obviously stress, doubt, and worry increase those visible signs of aging.

7. **You don't fit into your favorite jeans anymore. It's time to get back into shape.**

   Add 100 to 300 stress points then subtract them if you actually act on it.

   It is often assumed that dieting and exercising is a stressful and unpleasant experience. Instead, consider that taking care of your health can be a very enjoyable activity, and exercising is a great way to release stress as well as one of the best ways to maintain your physical and mental ability.

8. **You woke at 4:00 a.m. and discovered that you don't know your values in life anymore.**

   Add 300 stress points.

   You don't know who you are anymore or what you want out of life. You might want to find a meaning and a purpose, but first you need to redefine your values. Your values might be different in your forties from the ones you had in your twenties. Ultimately, you will have greater well-being if you can move to a stage of realizing what is important and worthwhile, but for now you feel stuck and it's challenging.

9. **You decide to give up your high-paying high-pressure job to collect old dolls. You develop a deep respect for antiquity and tolerance for poverty.**

   Add 200 financial stress points then subtract 200 stress points for following your passion.

   You create stress by creating a financial struggle, and you are leaving a job where you might have been comfortable in even though you complained about it all the time. But you can subtract those stress points and some more by finally pursuing your dream. One of my clients had to leave her job as technical writer in order to fulfill a dream to fix antique dolls by replacing their hair. She had to let go of her paradigm of what was required from her in order to financially support herself. The cost was high, the reward higher. Her finances suffer slightly from her choice, but she is thrilled that she's now following her passion, and since she has very specific skills, her business is growing exponentially.

If you reach 800 points or more, welcome to the world of the Feminine Midlife Crisis. There isn't a single component that will tell you what you are experiencing. Each cliché is painful in its own way, implying that as we get older, we are inevitably faced with loss, relationship problems, feelings of failure, and despair. If you're convinced by now that you're going through a midlife crisis, it might be worthwhile to work on the areas that concern you the most: your health, your relationships, your job, or your well-being. The midlife years span many decades, and even though the process is challenging, it creates positive growth and the outcome can be extremely rewarding.

Let's look at what is causing you stress. In order to do that, you must consider every aspect of your life. Life is like a diamond with eight facets. In order to shine, this diamond must let the light go through it. Even if only one facet is tarnished, the light will be blocked and the whole diamond will look dark and dull.

Now that you recognize the symptoms, it's time to change.

Life Self-Evaluation

The Rating Your Life quiz may have made you realize that you are facing real challenges but you don't know exactly what to do about them yet. To get a more precise idea about what you need to focus on, let's consider the eight main facets of life people tend to struggle with. How do you feel you are doing in the eight facets of life, with "one" being terrible to "ten" being wonderful? The list is not exhaustive, and you are welcome to create your own subcategory if necessary.

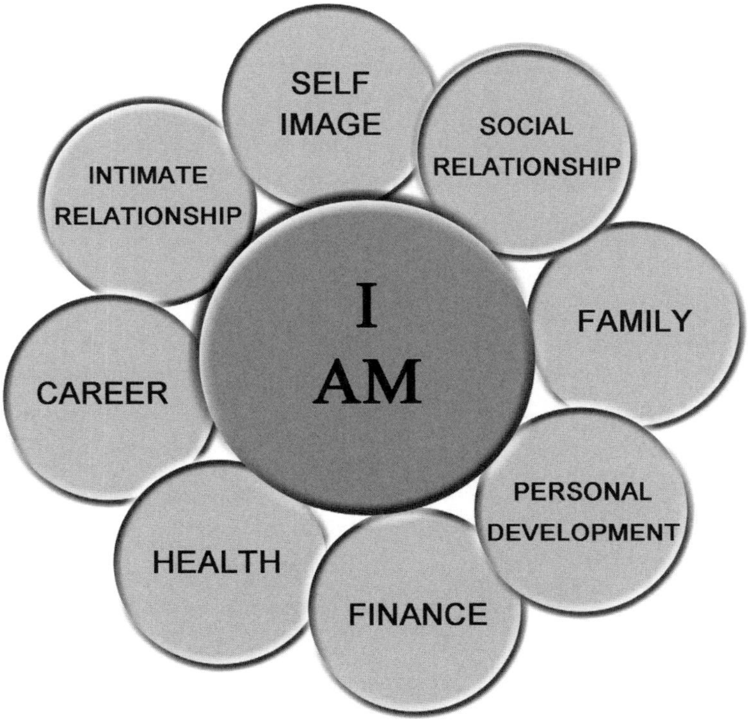

Family/Parenting	1 2 3 4 5 6 7 8 9 10
Personnel Development	1 2 3 4 5 6 7 8 9 10
Health	1 2 3 4 5 6 7 8 9 10
Personal Finance	1 2 3 4 5 6 7 8 9 10
Career/Profession	1 2 3 4 5 6 7 8 9 10
Self-Image	1 2 3 4 5 6 7 8 9 10
Intimate Relationship	1 2 3 4 5 6 7 8 9 10
Social Relationship	1 2 3 4 5 6 7 8 9 10

Consider your results. Are you doing great at work but your personal relationship is at a standstill? Do you have a great connection with your family but can't accept the way you look when you attend those family reunions? Whether the challenge is more about your health, your relationship, you career, or your finances...you've reached a dead end and feel confused or even stressed to the point of frustration.

Any stress you may experience expresses itself in your psyche but also in your body. Negative thoughts create tension in your brain. Your brain reacts by sending signals to your body ordering it to produce hormones according to what is needed to respond to the stress message. Those hormones change the chemical balance in your body. Your body experiences the chemical imbalance as unfavorable feelings: fear, worry, anger, sadness, etc. Those feelings will be associated with body sensations such as shoulder tension, headache, stomachache, shortness of breath, etc. The thoughts, emotions, and sensations will make you overall uncomfortable, and that will push you to respond and take action accordingly.

Thoughts
↓
Brain Stimulation
↓
Hormones
(testosterone, adrenaline, cortisol)
↓
Feelings
↓
Sensation
↓
Actions

Any stress you may experience expresses itself in your psyche but also in your body. As human beings, we tend to experience life and react to it according to six different levels of energy from the most negative or depressed Level 1 to the most positive and peaceful Level 6. The first two levels are mostly "catabolic energy" (negative energy). They are usually experienced during a time of stress. Levels 3 to 6 contain more a more "anabolic energy" (positive energy), which will be discussed in detail in the next chapters. Let's focus on the catabolic part for now. Everyone responds differently to stress, but those responses are coming from the reptilian and limbic part of our brain.

Catabolic energy triggers responses such as freeze, flight, or fight. It is a reactive energy essential to respond to dangerous situation, but it is draining energy in daily situations.

They are the freeze, flight, or fight responses. Catabolic energy is mostly draining and destructive. It expresses itself in our body by a release of cortisol and adrenaline. It creates stress and makes us reactive, fearful, victimized, defiant, etc. It triggers physical pain, weight gain or loss, and fatigue among other things. We experience what people describe as the "syndrome of the hamster in the spinning wheel," with circular thoughts keeping us awake at night and tense during the day.

The Energy Levels Pyramid[2]

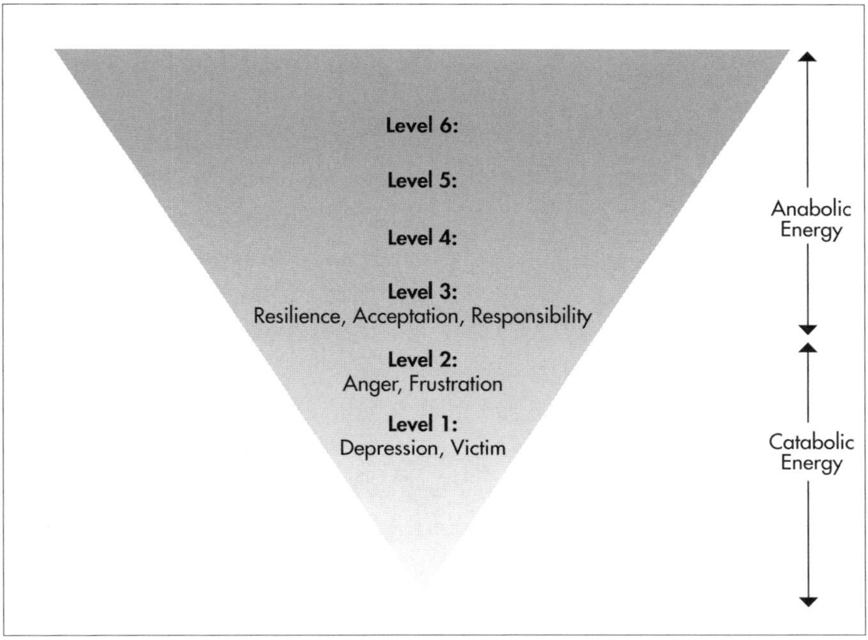

Level 1: The level has the lowest energy. At this level, we feel **victim to the situation**. At its lowest point, the statements going through the mind of women who are experiencing this type of energy are, "I feel depressed." "I can't function in any way." "It's my fault." "I am sad, lost . . ." At this level we don't have any energy—everything looks grim and hopeless. We feel like the situation is imposed on us, and we don't see any way out.

---

[2] Model inspired by the Energetic Self Perception chart - Energy Leadership: Transforming Your Workplace and Your Life from the Core – November 9, 2007 by Bruce D. Schneider

Level 2: This is the level of **anger or frustration**. It is a destructive level, since it is the level of conflict, argumentation, or frustration. We want to be right more than you want to change the situation. Surprisingly, this level may be required in order to change what we are experiencing during this period of transition. Being frustrated is the first step to letting go of what is not working for us anymore.

It is important to consider that while you may experience feelings associated with the various levels, you are not your feelings. They may seem to be your reality in life, but they are in fact the way we experience and interpret the reality—nothing more. Pay attention to the next time you experience one of those feelings. To help modify this perception, you may want to change the way you express it.

> **You are not your feelings:**
>
> Try to replace the statement "I am...(negative feeling)" by "I feel..."

Instead of saying, "I am sad, I am tired, I am upset..." why don't you try to say, "I feel sad, tired, and upset? "I am" tends to be a way to define who you are. It is your identity. "I feel" is just the way you experience a situation. It can be changed by altering your perception or sometimes waiting for the situation to change. Saying, "I am disappointed," feels definite. "I feel disappointed" opens the possibility for change.

Most of the world lives at Level 1 and Level 2 of energy. It affects the way we experience a situation but also the way we interact with others in our personal and professional relationships. Two people experiencing a Level 2 of energy will tend to argue. They will each try to be right, creating a situation of conflict. The duo Level 1–Level 2 is often seen in situations of offender-victim. A person feeling victimized is trying to find someone who will reconfirm his or her feeling of being a victim. In consequence, they might enter a relationship with someone who is abusive or injurious in any way, reconfirming the way they feel about themselves. In the same way, a dominant type will try to connect to someone who will be more submissive in order to feel superior and place the other under his or her control.

The only way to get out of these spirals of catabolic energy is to go to Level 3.

Level 3: This is the first level where we see the hint of a light. It is the level in which we try to look for the silver lining, the lesson in what we are experiencing. It also the level in which we start **taking responsibility** for our actions instead of blaming others. We might not yet know how but we want to get better, and we try to let go of the past and move on. A person experiencing Level 3 will try to find a solution to save herself instead of feeling under the burden of a situation. She might not always be able to sustain positivity, but she is trying. Usually, women capable of displaying a lot of Level 3-type of energy are considered resilient.

Let's find out what makes us experience catabolic energy, and, more importantly, how to move on from it.

Recognizing Your Blocks

There are many reasons you feel victimized of a person or of a situation. Don't blame yourself for who you are. Don't judge yourself. You are the person you are because of what happened in your life since the day you were conceived up to today. You may want to react differently, but until now, something has been preventing you from changing your perception of events. You have been stopped by what we call "blocks" or "saboteurs," also known as **GAIL: Gremlin[3], Assumption, Interpretation, Limited Belief**. Let's start from the lowest energy to the one with the highest power.

---

[3] According to Merriam-Webster, "gremlin" means:
grem·lin: a small imaginary creature that is blamed when something (such as a machine) does not work properly. In our case, it is the little negative voice in your head that tries to antagonize you.

Limited belief is this thing we believe to be true because a consensus says so. I will use the example of one of my clients who wanted who wanted to lose weight. She has heard over and over again that "It is extremely difficult, if not impossible, to lose weight after forty." She believed that until she decided to challenge this belief. Her answer to those negative voices became, "Says who?" Today I can tell you only one thing: There are no rules. Losing weight or taking care of your health can be seen as hard work or a fun project toward a better you. It will certainly be way more difficult to achieve your goal if you believe that what you are trying to do is impossible because of what you heard from others. Nutrition experts[4] explain that the way our body processes insulin changes as we age, and our metabolism slows down, but that doesn't mean we can't lose weight. Eating healthy, paying attention to the quality of what you put inside your body, choosing mostly natural ingredients, and enjoying our food instead of fighting it is essential to weight control.

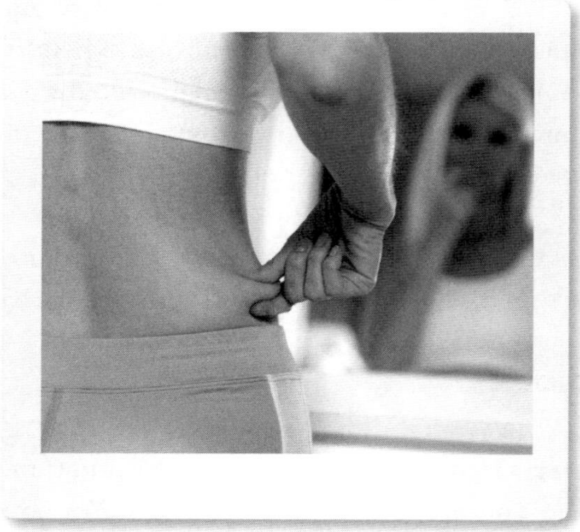

When talking about weight loss, there is no quick fix but a healthier way to look at food. Be patient with yourself, be aware, reframe your message about food, reach out for support from friends or professionals, and be selfish. Get your own opinions and challenge the limited beliefs. It is your body, it is your life, and you are the one in control of it. Learn to love it, be mindful, and take care of you first. Women are caretakers by nature, but we cannot take care of anyone well unless we first take care of ourselves.

---

[4] Dr. Rugh: Greenlite Medicine, Inc.
Lauri Beck: Territory Manager of Weight Watchers, Inc.

Interpretation is the opinion or a judgment you create about an event, person, or experience and believe to be true, such as, "He said this, I understood that." "He behaved that way because..."

How often do we let an interpretation dictate the way we react to a situation? Consider the case of this woman who has been making a presentation for her company. She was perfectly prepared, but during the presentation, her boss was rolling his eyes and by the end of it, he was almost asleep. That was how the woman interpreted what was going on. Frustrated, she asked for a meeting with her boss. As she expressed her feelings and her doubts about the quality of her presentation, he answered, "I was wearing new contact lenses and they were hurting my eyes. By the end of the presentation, it was so painful I had to close my eye, but I didn't want to leave. Your presentation was fantastic."

What we consider true is sometimes different than the truth.

When everything is good in your life, you see everything that happens in a positive light. When you don't feel so great, it seems like a lens is put in front of any emotion and colors them in a negative light.

Looking at situations objectively requires considering two very important laws: the Law of Polarity and the Law of Relativity. According to the **Law of Polarity**, you can always look at the same event in a positive way and in a negative way. Being fired from your job may in fact give you the opportunity to look for something different and closer to what you really wanted to do.

"We do not see the world as it is, we see it as we are."

- Anais Nin

Seeing your kids going to college means that you will miss them, but you know they are happy and now you have more time for yourself. It might be difficult, but finding the silver lining can help you get on the path to move on.

The **Law of Relativity** is recognizing that you can look at a specific situation in your life and always find someone who is in a worse, or better, situation. Sometimes when you feel down, it is helpful to realize that you have quite a few things that are actually working in your life.

Just pay attention to what is reality before making any major decision. Use your intuition, but don't forget to check with your logical-thinking brain that you are not making a hasty decision.

Assumption is an expectation that because something has happened in the past, it will happen again. It is a feeling that will prevent you from trying another time. If you feel that you tried over and over again to find a solution to a problem, why should it change the next time you try? If you have been on ten different diets without success, if you have been jumping from one frustrating job to another, if you think that whatever you try "he will never notice you because he never does," why should you try once more?

You cannot change what happens, but you can change your future. Like Einstein says, "Insanity is doing the same thing over and over again and expecting different results." But trying once more doesn't have to be synonymous with doing the same thing repeatedly. You might have to try doing things differently by using what you learned from your past experiences in order to expect a different outcome.

The **Gremlin** is your inner critic that tells you, in one way or another, that you are not good enough. Your gremlin tells you not to try, never take a risk, and always compromise by playing small. Your gremlin tells you that you are just not good enough to achieve your dreams. In my case, the gremlin was an ugly voice in my head that had repeated the same thing over and over again for years: "You are too much this or not enough that." This voice made me believe I was too fat, too tall, not smart enough, not pretty enough, that I didn't deserve to be happy, that I couldn't be myself and simply be happy with who I was. I heard many versions of it from my clients: "I am not beautiful, not smart, not lovable. I don't deserve my luck. Who am I to want more?" The imagination of the gremlin is limitless. It is your saboteur, the little devil on your shoulder who weighs tons, and the one who keeps you sleepless at night and crying in the morning.

Feeling 1: Alone by Fabienne Slama Bismuth

I realize I was the one who allowed this voice to get bigger and bigger. I fed this monster. I chose to feed it until he was able to eat me alive, until I didn't have energy left, until I was convinced I became what he told me I was *not enough this, too much that*. Once you consider the truth of what this monster is saying, you might realize how wrong it is, but when you are feeling down, this voice can be overbearing. Even if you recognize that it's just negative self-talk and not reality, you probably have listened to this voice for many years and it is extremely difficult to challenge it.

Today, I am aware of my gremlin and I acknowledge it. It is not an enemy. Most often, a gremlin was created when you were a kid and needed something or someone to protect you. It might have been the one who first told you not to talk in front of others because your classmates might make fun of you. It might have been the one who said you could be abandoned because your mom forgot to pick you up at school. Like in Chloe's case in Chapter 1, the gremlin might have been the one who told you that if you were to have fun, you might get punished. It might come from big traumas like abuse, or very small ones that didn't feel so small at the time they happened. Something stressful in the mind of a five- or six-year-old might not seem so significant now that you are an adult and you wonder why you even ever cared about it. However, this gremlin from your childhood is still influencing you today at the same level it did when you were a kid.

Many of my clients have a gremlin who is a perfectionist. Most of the time it came from what they had learned about—what was expected from them as a child at school or at home. Although being a perfectionist can be a good thing and is part of what makes them the successful women they are today, this perfectionism is preventing them from trying anything new because it might not be perfect at first, and regardless of what they try, it is never going to be good enough.

Destroying a gremlin is not a good idea nor it is possible. Your gremlin is energy and, like energy, it cannot be destroyed. It can be transformed and this energy can be used to motivate you. A perfectionist gremlin can push you to perfect your skill and work hard toward improvement. If it becomes cumbersome, send it to another task.

When sculpting, I often have a hard time knowing when to stop working on my piece. Each time I hear this voice saying that what I am creating will never be good enough, I kick my perfectionist saboteur out from my head and send it perform a very simple and tedious imaginary task somewhere else. I imagine it going across the world very far away from me, keeping busy with its own business of annoying someone else, and leaving me alone and in peace. Imagination is a powerful tool and it will make your gremlin do what you ask it to do while you actually work on your project with peace of mind. It sounds like a fun solution and actually is a very powerful one. Your imagination is a powerful tool and it will make your gremlin do what you ask it to do.

Feeling 2: In a Box by Fabienne Slama Bismuth

You can visualize your gremlin and transform the image you draw in your mind as a less scary one by changing its color, the pitch of it voice, and its size. Once it is less scary, you can confront it and tell it that you choose a different message than the negative one it is sending to you.

A tool you might want to consider is to **name your gremlin**. Choose a name that is significant to you but is not the name of a person you know. One client who used to feel that her house would never be clean enough called her gremlin "Messup." She drew Messup on a piece of paper. He was this ugly ball of dust, a scary little monster. Once she identified what it looked like to her, she start considering what she yearned for in her life and couldn't get because she was spending her time cleaning her house. She missed fun time with her kid, connection with her husband, and peace of mind among other things. The next time Messup showed its ugly face, she looked at her drawing, thanked it for its lessons, and looked at the other side of the paper where she had written everything she wanted to do with the time when she was not cleaning. Then she made her choice.

Feeling 3: Out of the Box by Fabienne Slama Bismuth

During my midlife crisis, my gremlin kept me stuck, fearful in a box. Once I chose to let it go, I became free.

Identifying the Old Message of Self-Doubts

In the mist of a midlife crisis, you may not know yourself anymore. You are under stress. You experience catabolic energy at its maximum and a lot of negative feelings start invading your brain. Fear is usually at the forefront, as well as guilt of not having done what you should have done, sadness for the relationship you have or don't have anymore, and anger toward your partner, your boss, yourself, tiredness, boredom, frustration, etc. Those feelings of self-doubt are created by the messages your gremlin has been repeating in your head. You have been accepting those messages as part of your identity in compliance with your old paradigm.

Those are example of negative words we use to define ourselves. If you think you "are" one of those words, how do you think it affects the way you behave?

Lazy	Manipulative	Self-doubting
Fearful	Victim	Greedy
Insecure	Confrontational	Unmotivated
Selfish	Bored	Boring
Not good enough	Uncaring	Too sensitive
Not smart enough	Self-centered	Unsuccessful
Not attractive	Too aggressive	Withdrawn
Unsatisfied	Always worrying	Dull life
Ugly	Too old	

It's time you change those messages. They are not serving you. They are part of the past and the only way to move to the new beginning you want is to end with your old paradigm.

Unfortunately, it is not always easy to change your old believes and there is a good reason for that.

Why Is It so Difficult to Change?

Only twenty percent of our thoughts are conscious. That means that eighty percent are unconscious. Our body acts according to what our brain tells it to do, which is influenced at eighty percent by our unconscious system.

Most of the tasks we accomplish in our daily life on the unconscious level are essential for survival, from breathing, to sitting up straight, or

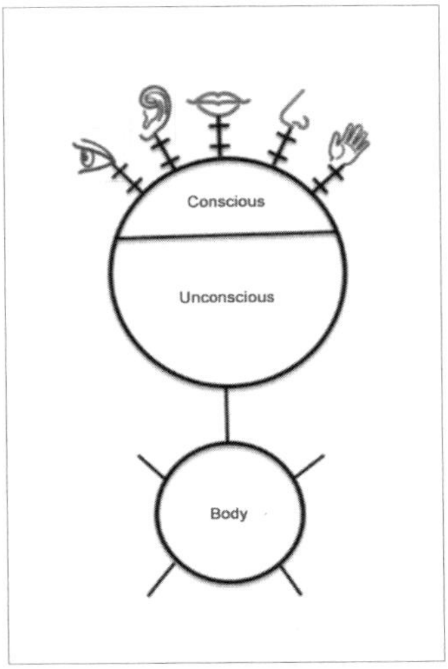

putting one foot in front of the other when walking. We had to learn some of those skills as an infant, but now can accomplish them without thinking about them. The way we react to a situation also depends on the message sent by our unconscious or subconscious brain.

Our subconscious is mostly governed by our paradigm—our experience in life, what was given to us by our parents, grandparents, society—and it reacts in a very basic way:

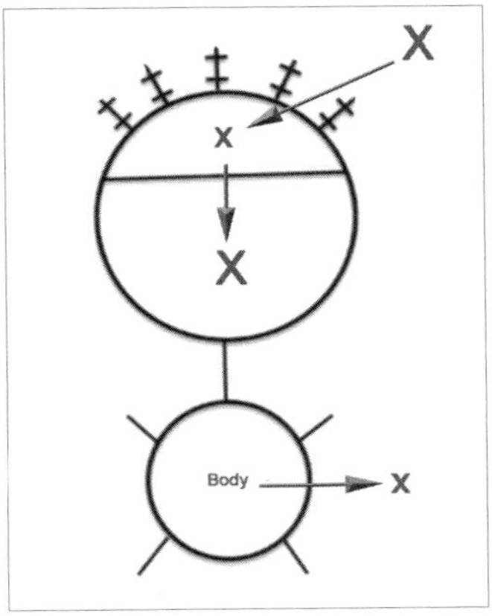

I like it. My system feels in agreement. I can breathe comfortably, my shoulders are relaxed, I smile . . .

I dislike it. My system is upset. My heart beat is faster, I feel anxious, my muscles tighten up . . .

Each thought and memory in your subconscious brain is anchored there because a particular feeling and sensation is attached to it. This feeling can be positive or negative. In general, familiarity is considered by our system as safe. Our system likes familiarity and hates the unknown. Even if it's a situation that most people would not consider as positive, your unconscious might be used to it and feel good about it. That is one reason that someone may have such a hard time leaving an abusive relationship. It's also why something that may be perceived as a good thing, like getting a promotion at work, might create a lot of stress.

If you are used to situation *X*, this situation will create a thought *x*. This thought will create a feeling *X* at your subconscious level, and your body will react accordingly and behave accordingly.

Now, imagine that you are bringing a totally different idea or a different situation *Y*. This new situation will create a thought about what is happening *y*. Your subconscious is still used to the idea *X*. Your body reacts to this usual idea *x*. Your brain gets confused, because there is a conflict between the conscious and the unconscious level, and this creates an uncomfortable sensation in your body.

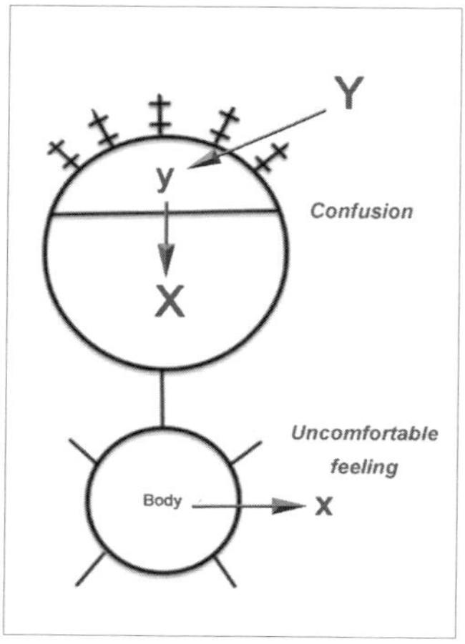

Let's look to how this is impacting women during a midlife crisis. You are in your forties or fifties. Your life is changing, or you want it to change, because you are no longer in agreement about what was your life until now. You have to let go of your past. Everything that was your life until now was known and recognized by your system as safe. Now you are introducing new ideas, new concepts, and your subconscious is just doing its job of keeping you secure by triggering a more or less uncomfortable sensation.

You have two choices: go back to what is known, or challenge it. Challenging it is not that easy. One of my friends was in an abusive relationship for the past twenty-five years. She finally managed to find the courage to leave it. She moved out of her place and tried to look for a job. Unfortunately, her body had learned from her childhood that "women like us don't divorce." Her emotionally abusive and manipulative husband had pushed over and over in her mind that she would "never be capable of taking care of herself on her own."

She tried very hard to pass this belief and chase her gremlin, but after four months of struggle, going back to her submissive role felt better. So, she went back to her past miserable life. She couldn't make it. Maybe one day she will challenge it again if she can get the support to help her go through her blocks.

Courage is risking the known for the unknown, the familiar for the unfamiliar, the comfortable for the uncomfortable arduous pilgrimage to some unknown destination. One never knows whether he or she will be able to make it or not. Courage is looking at your fears and accepting them, then deciding to jump and move forward. It is a gamble, but only the gamblers will experience the life they desire. What do you have to do to pass your blocks, pass your fears, send your gremlin away, and move to your better life?

Courage is looking at your fears and accepting them. Then decide to push beyond what feels safe.

When a new idea *Y* presents itself and is not in congruence with your paradigm, it will feel uncomfortable and you will tend to reject it at first. Your first reaction is fear and sounds something like this: "I can't do that. I am not capable of leaving my good-paying job to follow my passion. I can't travel around the world on my own. I can't leave my marriage even if I am unhappy. I can't stay in my marriage and be who I want to be. I can't get used to my kids going away and not being a mom anymore. I have a good enough life. Who am I to want more?"

The only way to change your perspective at the unconscious level is to modify the thoughts, the feelings associated to it, and the way your body reacts when you think about the new situation.

Acting on any of those three elements—**thought, feeling,** and **sensation**—will change your perception of the situation. Modifying the three elements will allow the best chance of a permanent change.

When you create a new idea, your subconscious is not ready to accept it, but since your subconscious is responsible for eighty percent of your actions, it is very important that it comes onboard. Here are few ways to make your conscious and your subconscious accept new ideas. The concept is always the same: You need to lower the energy of the bad feelings and increase the energy of the good feelings. It is very simple, but at the same time, it is hard work.

The first step is to stop being scared of your feelings. They are just emotions. We may have been told that emoting, crying, screaming, or getting anxious is "bad," but it is not the case. As unpleasant as it is, a negative emotion is just an emotion like a good one could be.

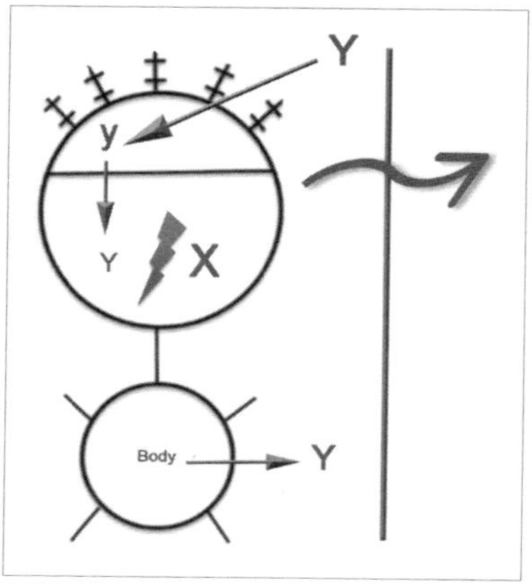

Feeling sad, tired, nervous, angry, or guilty are all feelings. My mentor used to say, "Feeling your feelings is healthy." Don't try to fight your emotions.

If you actually accept that they are there for a reason and that they are temporary, you will have won half of the battle. The reason they are so unpleasant is because each emotion creates a body sensation.

To illustrate that, let me ask you to play along with me. Close your eyes and think about a bad memory. Bring the image to your brain. Imagine you are re-experiencing this very bad time in your life. Create the storyline in your mind. Face the person who caused you pain. Are you there? Great. Now scan your body. Do you feel the shortness of breath? The tension in your jaw? The pain in your belly? The pressure in your heart? If

> To change the way you respond to a situation, you need to change the thought/feeling/sensation response to this situation.

yes, good. It is normal. If no, don't worry; some people have a hard time getting in touch with their feelings but will get to it with practice. It may be counter-intuitive to relieve painful feelings, but the only way to deeply release them is to look at them once more for what they are: a lesson in your life, an experience, a part of your story, and choosing to let them go once and for all. Let me explain how to do that.

The best way to release the feeling associated with this scene will be to focus on the physical pain (heart break, stomach pain, weight on the shoulder, throat constricted...) and move the energy: jump, run, pound on a pillow, throw something against a wall, cry, laugh, breathe deeply . . . do whatever it takes to lower the physical sensation. Usually the sensation will go away after one to two minutes. It might be intense and scary, but I can promise that it will not last.

According to neuroscientist and neuroanatomist Jill Bolte Taylor, ninety seconds is the longest amount of time that an emotion can last in anyone's body. After those ninety seconds, the chemicals elements (cortisol, adrenaline, etc.) released by your body in response to a feeling are totally flushed out.

Most of the time people choose to hold onto it and stay angry after the initial ninety seconds of chemical-physiological response by reliving the story of what happened in their mind. What would be different if you chose to let go of it and shut off the anger after ninety seconds and be at peace? It is our choice to consciously or unconsciously rethink the thoughts that re-stimulates the circuit. Letting go of the physical sensation will help you see the feeling more objectively, and hopefully it will make it possible to change it and change the thoughts

associated with this feeling. That is why exercise can help tremendously in a period of stress. Besides the health component of exercising regularly in your forties and fifties, moving your body and consequently your energy will lower the feeling associated with stress.

This may look very complex, but it is actually simpler than it seems. *Anna is fifty-three. She has been working for the same company for the past eighteen years but she feels that she is not appreciated at work. Changing feels very scary to her, and at the same time, she really feels that her boss is bullying her and she can't stand it anymore. The main reason she doesn't want to leave her current job is that she thinks she will never find a new job. She feels like a victim of the situation. Her gremlin is telling her that she is not smart enough and that she has no value. Those thoughts are triggering mostly anger and sadness. This situation has been governing her life during the past eighteen months, and at this point, her body is physically reacting to the stress. Her blood pressure is getting dangerously higher, and she experiences constant pain in her joints and neck. She is continuously tired and can barely move because she has "no energy." Now that her health is a concern, she is even more terrified at the idea of looking for another job because she needs the health coverage this one provides.*

We worked together, and Anna experienced a shift after a couple of sessions. Once she accepted to face her feelings and actually let them go, which she did by using the technique of Emotional Healing Therapy[5]*, she started feeling better. Within a couple of weeks, she had enough energy to rewrite her résumé. After a month, Anna had sent her résumé to a couple of headhunters. Two months after our first talk, Anna had a new job in a new company. After another month, she was taking care of her health in a totally different way and is training for a half marathon. Today, Anna is way more relaxed, her health improved, and she is more positive about her future.*

---

[5] Emotional Healing Therapy: Combination of coaching, regression hypnotherapy, NLP and other techniques. Should be learned with a professional. Go to www.pathtoperfectself.com to schedule a session.

Anna's case is one of the many examples I had the chance to observe in my practice, and even if the story differs from one person to another, the steps to get better are mostly the same.

- Recognize your feelings and decide that you really want to challenge what you were accepting as true until now. You cannot change unless you want it.
- Identify the thoughts and the sensation experienced from your body.
- Release the body sensation.
- Address the feeling associated. At this step, if someone else has been part of the source of this feeling, you might want to try to forgive this person(s).

Tools to Let Go of Negative Feelings

There are many ways to let go of negative feelings. I will just give a short description of the main tools you can easily use on your own.

I repeat, the first thing to remember is DO NOT IGNORE FEELINGS. Take the time to acknowledge them and accept that they are sending you a message to pay attention. If those feelings are strong, you will have to face them one way or another. Ignoring them will just delay the time when you do that. Feelings express themselves in your body. Expressions such as "heartbreak," "pain in the neck," and "butterflies in the stomach" come from the way your feelings get expressed at your body level. If you don't acknowledge your feelings, they will impact your body, and the catabolic energy might make you sick over time.

The best way to let go of feelings is to MOVE YOUR ENERGY. This can be done in many different ways:

- **Breathe.** Deep breath will calm down your emotions and allow more clarity.

- **Be in the present** by breathing deeply and meditating.
- **Exercise.** Move your body—dance, run, punch, jump, stretch—any movement, preferably active, tiring, and with a sense of rhythm will help.
- **Shake.** Let your body tremble if it needs to. This technique is called TRE (Trauma Release Exercise) and is used on PTSD (Post-Traumatic Stress Disorder) patients by the military. Under a major stress, your body may naturally let the excess energy express itself in the form of a tremble. It might seem scary, but it is a natural function of your system. Just let your body move any way it wants and acknowledge that it is simply a way to let catabolic energy escape your body.
- **Tap.** This technique is based around the principles of EFT (Emotional Freedom Technique) and NLP (Neuro-Linguistic Programming) consisting on expressing what you would like to see changing while tapping along meridians points on your body.
- **Talk**. Talk therapy has been a pillar of emotional release for many years. Traditional talk therapy tends to allow the client to express feelings freely and find a solution by thinking about it. It is essential not to ignore the subconscious level. Sometimes wanting to change is not enough when your subconscious is not onboard.
- **Emotional Healing Therapy.** This is an exceptionally powerful combination of tapping, talk therapy, and self-hypnosis. You need to work with a professional at first who will teach you the skill necessary to do it on your own.
- **Express yourself** by writing, drawing, sculpting, etc. Creativity can be a wonderful outlet.

THERE IS NO MAGIC BULLET. You might have experienced certain feelings for months if not for years. Do not be disappointed if your life doesn't change overnight. It usually takes three weeks to change a habit, but there is no rule about how much time releasing a feeling takes. The more you accept that it is just a feeling linked to a story called "your past" and that it is not defining who you are, the easiest it will be to release it.

DO NOT FORGET TO REPLACE YOUR NEGATIVE FEELINGS BY POSITIVE ONES. An empty space is created once you empty your pit of negative thoughts. This space in your brain will be filled up with whatever presents itself. If you let it empty, there is a big chance negative experiences will fill up your pit with catabolic energy. Once you release a negative feeling, take the time to replace it by a positive one. Think about a part of your life you are grateful for by meditating, repeating a positive mantra, or doing something that you enjoy doing. Focus on the positive elements, remind yourself of all the things that are good, and take the time to enjoy what you have and all your positive attributes.

ACCEPT that once you let go of what you don't want, you might have to spend some time learning about what you want. Most of the time we let go of negative feelings and we are just left with a sensation of nothingness, but after a period of intense sadness or anger, you might feel a burst of energy. Don't be fooled by this **pendulum effect**. The goal is not for you to be overexcited but more to feel at peace and emotionally strong.

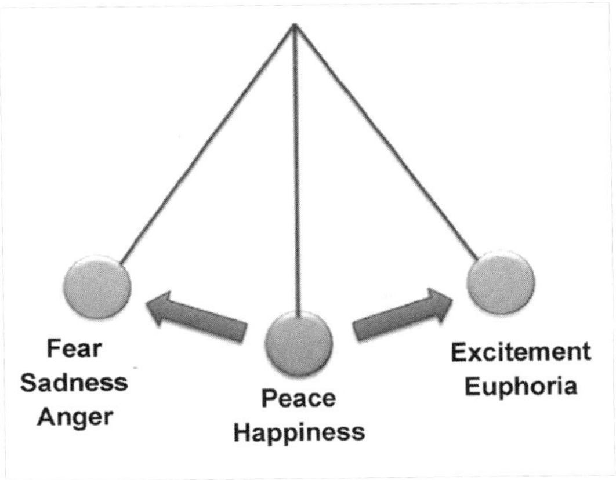

To reach this level, you will probably have to face a period when nothing really happens until you define the new you. This period feels like a neutral zone, a limbo.

CHAPTER 3

The Limbo–The Paradigm Shift

*"God grant me the serenity to accept
the things I cannot change,
the courage to change the things I can
and the wisdom to know the difference."*

- Reinhold Niebuhr

"The end" allowed you to let go of some of your old beliefs, of your paradigms. Now, you are entering "the limbo" where you get to define yourself. Unfortunately, as a midlife woman, this second phase can be extremely distressing. You had to let go of your old identity and you are confused about who you are. You were faced with many voluntary or involuntary changes: divorce, empty nest, career change, relocation, illness, or death of your parents, or some of your friends may have left because they don't agree with your decisions. You letting go of your identity—the old you—was already painful enough, but until you rebuild your new identity, you will be experiencing limbo. Disorientation is meaningful and essential to move on further, but it isn't enjoyable. It is a time of confusion and emptiness.

Once everything we knew is dismantled, once we have looked at the rules by which we use to live our lives and decided to challenge them, we may lose any sense of direction for a while. On one hand, things are full of promises; on the other hand, they lack meaning. On one hand, your kids are grown up or almost grown up, leaving you with a lot of extra time; on the other end, your parents are getting old and you might feel the pressure of the years. On one hand, being forty and fifty can be just the beginning, considering our life expectancy; on the other hand, it sometimes feels like the beginning of the end. Oscar Wilde said, "When the gods wish to punish us, they answer our prayers." If you arrived in your forties and have realized all your dreams, you may ask yourself, "Is this it?" And if you have failed to realize them, you have to face "the nevers": the fact that you might never have children of your own, be famous, become a surgeon, etc. You might change some of your nevers, while some you might have to accept the way they are.

"Life offers neither problems nor challenges, only opportunities."

- Bruce Schneider

Feminine renaissance and the major life changes associated with it can disengage us from the context in which we have known ourselves. The causes for those changes make little difference on whether the person experiencing the transition will have a hard time dealing with it or not. The transition can even be the result of a period of time where apparently nothing major happened. Something even more surprising for an outside observer is that changes initially desired and initiated by the person can trigger the biggest challenges later on. Transitions and endings can be welcomed. They might come from a change that was long due, like getting fired from this job that they didn't like anymore, or seeing a long-time unpleasant relationship end. Whatever the source of the problem, it is not the breaking of the old paradigm that forces us to design a new one. Instead, as long as the old system is working, it is very difficult to imagine an alternative way of life and an alternative identity. But once the process has begun, we are engaged in an inexorable changing pattern. If we are not ready for a real transformation, we will go back to our old, familiar and comfortable habits. But if we let go of the past, we will enter a new phase leading toward development and renewal.

"The only thing that is constant is change."

- Heraclitus

Before any change occurred, life was pretty simple; who we thought we were determining the way we acted in life, what we were doing, and how we were doing it. Once this pattern is challenged, voluntarily or not, we have to reevaluate how we are behaving. If we continue acting the same way over and over again there will be no change. The only way to redefine who you are is actually to STOP and EVALUATE what you are doing, why you are doing what you are doing, LEARN from that experience, and DECIDE to eventually create a NEW YOU.

The way you define yourself—the words used to describe who you are—determine your self-image. Remind yourself of the words of self-doubts identified in the previous chapter. It is important to identify your old rules and the old message you may have given to yourself until now and that you challenge this message whether it comes from you or from somebody else.

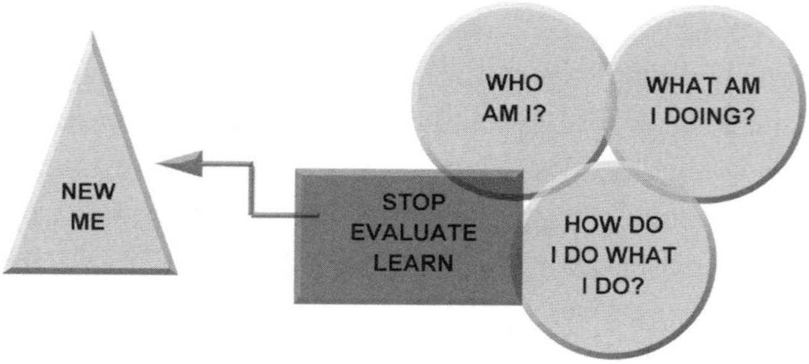

In order to challenge your old beliefs, you had to let go of the past. In order to create new beliefs, you have to accept that what you experienced until now doesn't define you. It is just a story that happens to be your story. In life, we all go through highs and lows, illness and pain, physical and emotional traumas. An event that can seem dramatic at first may be seen as a positive episode when you look back at it months later. A purpose can often be found in what happens to us even though it may be difficult to recognize at that time. While human traumas include pain, we have a choice on how we view it. What would be different for you if you could see life like a perfect adventure, like a game that cannot be won or lose but only played?

"Pain is inevitable. Suffering is optional."

- Haruki Murakami

We create our world through interpretations of reality. We are the ones making those interpretations. We can't change the facts, but we can change our interpretation of them. We can decide to be at the effect of our life or at the cause of our life. Most people think they are at the effect of their life, but the only way to change this perception is to accept that you are responsible of each aspect of your destiny. That means that you are also responsible for the results of each aspect of your life: your health, your relationships, your

> We can be at the effect of our life or chose to be at the cause of our life.

feelings, your career, etc. That doesn't mean that you are the cause of a difficult situation. It simply means that no one but you is responsible for what you are experiencing, and you are the one who can choose the way you react to it.

Overall, our experience in life will greatly depend on our interpretation of the facts, and it is okay to fall down, to "fail," as long as we learn from the experience and stand up again.

The Role of Forgiveness

Forgiveness is a very powerful but often misunderstood concept. Forgiving doesn't mean to let the person who hurt you off the hook. It is more about realizing that, as terrible as what this person did to you, it is about them and their journey in life and not about you. Your abuser didn't hurt you because you were *less than* him but that it was what he was doing at this time in his life considering his circumstances and his level of consciousness.

Forgiving is not about setting the other person free but more about setting yourself free by removing yourself from the power of this person. As you are trying to forgive, you might take this opportunity to forgive the persons around you who could have help you but didn't. You might even have to forgive yourself for not being able to get out of a painful situation earlier, or for not having been able to forgive until now and being a captive victim of your resentment until now.

"When you forgive, you in no way change the past - but you sure do change the future."

- Bernard Meltzer

You have been a prisoner of the circumstances and may have only been able to stay a prisoner of your past until now. You did the best you could at that time, and still today you do the best you can at your own level of consciousness. But now it's time to let go of this past, of this story. It is just a story, and even though it is your story, you have no power in changing what was already written. You can just change what will be written from now on. You have the power, so make it a beautiful one.

"The greatest freedom is the freedom of choice."

- *Bruce Schneider*

Forgiving is also a way to release catabolic energy and increase positive or anabolic energy. Once we start experiencing more Level 3 energy, we become able to accept our current situation. We let go of our role as a victim and we free ourselves from some, if not all, of the anger and frustration that was controlling our lives. When we are able to forgive, we are actually acting on a Level 4 of energy. We start looking at the situation from the other's point of view. It is at this level that the little girl, who is now an adult, might decide to take care of her elderly parents who used to abuse her on a regular basis. Not because she wants to forget, but because she doesn't want to keep the pain alive. Instead of looking at the abusive parent, she now looks at this old person who needs her support, and she decides to let go of her role of a victim and of her anger to actually express some compassion.

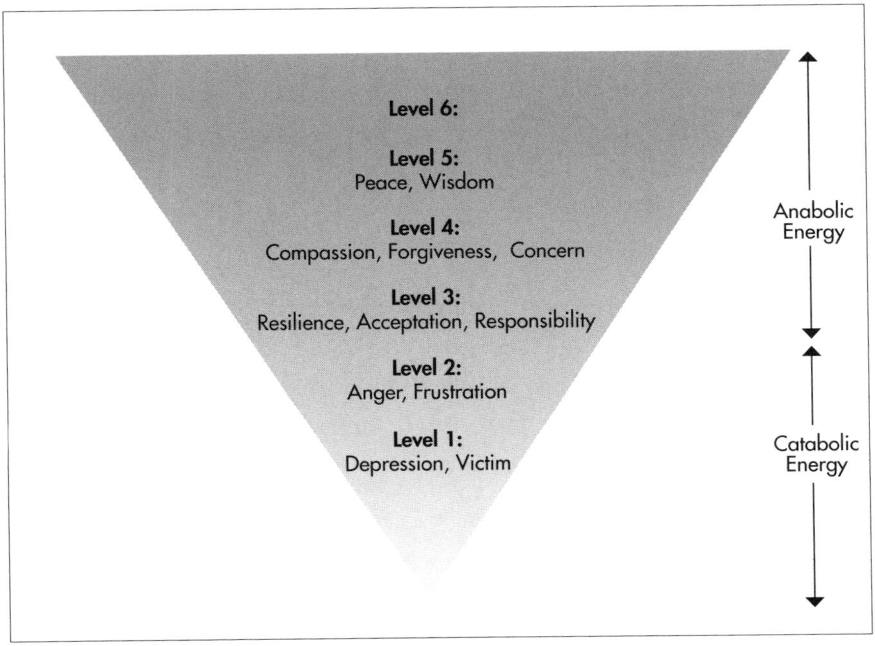

Forgiveness is often essential in a period of redefinition of one's identity. How can you redefine yourself as a powerful, strong human being if you still feel being the victim of your abuser?

There are many types of people you might want to forgive in your midlife. The most obvious is the physical or sexual abuser, but there are also the husbands who cheated, the one who never expressed how valuable you are, the coworker who humiliated you in front of the company, or the boss who didn't give you the raise eventhough you deserve it. Instead of lingering in this Level 1–Level 2 energy, taking responsibility of your own action (Level 3) and looking at the situation through the other's eyes (Level 4) will ultimately bring you to the next step: the new beginning, your rebirth;peaceful and strong.

In relationships, we usually attract our exact match (victim-victim) or our complementary (victim—abuser or victim—helper). We often attract our mirror, the person who will bring the best or the worst out of us.

We create codependency according to our needs. The average energy of a couple (relationship) is the average energy of each element of the couple. In a group, the majority of the group often entrains the lowest energy element. Since we have no power in making the other one change, the only control we have on changing a situation is to actually modify the way we react to it. If we don't like the life we have, the job we do day after day, our partner, and our role, we can either complain or take action.

"We have thoughts, feelings, and emotions, but we are not our thoughts, feelings, or emotions."

- *Frances Vaughn*

The Next Steps

Entering the neutral zone or limbo, you hopefully challenged your paradigm, were able to forgive those who hurt you, and let go of your own degrading self-definition. Then began this incubation period that seems really long because nothing major happened. You stay there as long as necessary to find the energy to confront the next step. Some women describe themselves in this period as "numb" and "inactive."

To me, the stage of limbo felt like a train had just hit me and went by. I had seen the end of my past, my family, my house, my childhood dreams, and I was still very sore. Entering the limbo, I knew who I was not anymore, but I didn't know who I was becoming. It was a very strange period that I had to revisit a few times, again and again, since a transition is not a straight line but more like an onion. I got the first layer out, abandoned everything I believed in (letting-go phase), felt immobile and powerless (limbo phase), then got better and started seeing a light at the end of the tunnel (rebirth phase). This tunnel had been the darkest one, but there were a few other ones and different layers to address. I got scared when I saw myself slipping up again into catabolic energy, but this time I was ready. By having experienced my first transition, by having to lose everything once and getting over it, I knew I had the power within me to get over it. I had done it once and I had the tools to let go of my catabolic energy. So, I went back to Level 1 once more and climbed back the energy levels one by one.

During this second journey, I didn't linger in the "letting go" phase since I had already let go of so many things, nor did I try to escape the sadness, the fear, and the anxiety by ignoring the feelings. I actually embraced them as a learning experience and a way to process, and I spent more time doing nothing to change the situation. It was not the best sensation. What seemed at first was like a period when nothing happened actually became a time to redefine my values, my priorities, and who I really wanted to be.

Defining your values and your beliefs is fundamental to move to the next phase. Don't be afraid if it takes weeks or months. Sometimes doing nothing is the best you can do to create a solid base for your future. Here are few exercises that should help you in this process.

Define Your Values

Circle your top five values

Accomplishment	Self-care	Loyalty	Self-care
Abundance	Excellence	Nature	Self-expression
Achievement	Family	Openness	Self-mastery
Adventure	Flexibility	Orderliness	Self-protection
Altruism	Freedom	Personal growth	Self-realization
Autonomy	Friendship	Partnership	Sensuality
Avoidance of conflict	Fulfillment	Physical appearance	Service
Beauty	Fun	Power	Spirituality
Clarity	Holistic living	Privacy	Trust
Commitment	Honesty	Professionalism	Truth
Communication	Humor	Recognition	Vitality
Community	Integrity	Respect	Other
Connecting to others	Intimacy	Romance	
Creativity	Joy	Safety	
Emotional health	Leadership	Security	

You have your own opinion of yourself and your own self-talk, but it is also important to take the time to find out how people around you perceive who you are. How do you think people would describe you? How do people actually describe you? Take the time to find five adjectives people might use to describe you. Then call a few friends and family members and ask them to give five adjectives that they think would define who you are. You might be surprised.

Intimates		Friends/Coworkers		Strangers/ Acquaintance	
Belief	Real	Belief	Real	Belief	Real

Take the most positive words from those lists, the ones that resonate the most with who you think you are or want to be. Then make a list of your main attributes and gifts.

Identify the key descriptors of who you are according to your values and those attributes. Transform them in "I am" statements, and write them in order of importance. Then take the time to reflect on what it means to you to have this attribute or to live according to this or that value. This exercise helps you get a strong base to define who you are. You already let go of your old rules and now you hopefully identified your new ones. You are strong enough to defy your gremlin or to challenge the people who say you can't or you shouldn't do something for one reason or another. Now that you have a better understanding of who you are, it's time to take the first step out of the limbo zone and define who you want to be.

CHAPTER 4

Your Rebirth

*"If you want to be happy,
put your effort into controlling the sail,
not the wind."*

- Anonymous

Life is a journey of becoming and growing. Each moment describes who you are and gives you the opportunity to decide if it's who you want to be. Setting goals is a way to get motivated, and more than the realization of those goals, the enjoyment of the journey itself is actually the best measure of success. You don't have to wait until the universe decides of your fate. On the contrary, by trying to create your best future according to your vision, you gain power and freedom over circumstances that are not under your control.

You attract and create your world. If you focus on the lack—failing relationships, not finding work, not having enough—then that is what you will see, and that is what will come back to you. Instead of brooding on what *was*, consider what *is*. From there create what *can be* and choose the world you

> You are the artist of your life and your future is a blank canvas.

want to live in. Focus on the positive, on moving forward, and abundance will come to you.

Living an abundant life begins with believing in an abundant world. It's time to design the future you would like for yourself and make decisions from a position of curiosity, knowing that everything can become an opportunity.

"Energy attracts like energy."

- Law of Attraction

You are not at the effect of your life. You have always been at choice. You cannot decide every aspect of your life, but you are the one who gets to choose the way you react to it. Life happens, with its ups and downs, and losing your identity not long ago can actually be the best opportunity you've ever had. What I described in the previous chapters is not easy work. The pain you experienced was real. You had to let go of many beliefs about who you were, and you may even have had to reevaluate some of your values. But today is the day when you can actually start painting your own life on your own canvas. What would you like it to look like? If I gave you a pack of clay to create a figure representing who you would like to be, what would you want it to look like today?

Feeling 4: So Fashion! Take the first step...
by Fabienne Slama Bismuth

A few years ago, I made a series of small sculptures without heads and arms—powerless and unable to think of a solution. I was so depressed at that time that I didn't even notice that they were just the expression of how I was feeling. How would it feel to create a woman standing tall, moving forward toward her future? Let me state the obvious here: The only way to start this journey toward accomplishing your goal is to take the first step.

The Range of Engagement

Start this journey by changing the words you use to describe the situation you are in. It is extremely difficult, if not impossible, to accomplish something if you think you have no power and no choice. When you feel depressed, everything looks so difficult. Every goal seems so far. When a client calls me feeling hopeless of her life and of her future, the first step is to create a reaction. Usually, this reaction will come in the form of frustration. You might say, "I need to do something about it." Sentences like, "I hate feeling like that," or "I need to change," are actually a step in the right direction. It might be a small step, but it is a step. As long as it feels like a "need," you won't appreciate that you are really at choice, and every move you might make in the direction of your goal will be effortful. *I need to* get back into shape is different than *I want to* get back into shape.

In the first case, you will make the efforts to do what you have to do, but they will feel like a battle against yourself. As soon as you accept that nobody is forcing you to make this decision but yourself, the process will be way easier. "I need to diet and exercise" might change to say, "I have to eat healthier and move if I want to be there for my kids, feel better in my body, and fit in this cute red dress I just bought." There are many ways to see a goal. After all, you are at choice. If you decide to live a healthier lifestyle, it

is because you have something to gain from it. Just take the time to realize what you will get from achieving your goal. How will you feel once you can do what you want to do? Once the "What's in it for Me" (WIFM) is stronger than the "What does it cost me," you will feel that you are choosing the best alternative for you. You will feel way more power in knowing that this is under your control after all, and the results are worth the efforts.

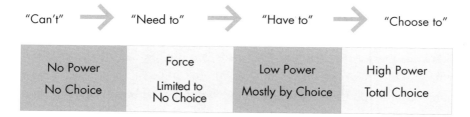

"Can't" → "Need to" → "Have to" → "Choose to"

"Can't"	"Need to"	"Have to"	"Choose to"
No Power No Choice	Force Limited to No Choice	Low Power Mostly by Choice	High Power Total Choice

This can be applied to any situation you are struggling with. Whether you want to lose weight, gain weight, run a marathon, quit your job, get into a new relationship, create your company, go on a six-month trip around the world, or achieve whatever dream you have, you are the master of your destiny. As long as there is no absolute physical limitation, you can do what you want to do.

The more anabolic energy is introduced, the less fighting or flying appears as a response to a situation. If your engagement toward change is low, you will consider your goal with very low energy and enthusiasm. You might even resist to any change or collaboration. In consequence, it will be very difficult, if not impossible, to take action.

If you feel that you are forced to make an effort but that your enthusiasm is limited or disrupted by a chaotic collaboration, you might be able to forcefully move toward your goal, but it might feel painful and challenging. For example, if your boss asks you to accomplish a task that you would like to accomplish but feel that you don't have the appropriate knowledge or support, you might be able to put it together, but it will require time and energy.

Now, let's imagine you feel like you have to accomplish something that is not in alignment with what you would like to do but you know that you have the capacity to do it. You can accomplish it. It might feel dreadful, and you might drag your feet, but you can push yourself to do it. Of course, this might not be sustainable and long-term unless you change your attitude toward this task.

The only way you will feel fully engaged and capable of taking action is to choose to take action, have total commitment and focus to finish what you have started. In order to shift things in your life, it is important to know exactly what you want, why you want it, how you want it and recognizing that you have the capacity of accomplishing what you want. It might require some external help or support, or some modification of your daily routine, but if you are fully engaged and able to recognize your skill and gifts, you will be almost unstoppable.

Where Are You Now?

The next part of this book will be very hands-on. I suggest having a notebook to work on it. It is your project, and writing it down will make it more tangible.

Being self-aware allows you to understand and appreciate how you think, feel and react. By recognizing where you are in life, you can work toward getting where you want to be. In the first part of this book, we looked in details at what has been blocking you, or preventing you from achieving your dreams. We looked at what you don't want anymore. We then took the time to consider the values and beliefs that are essential to you. Let's now identify what your personal strengths are and which skills you would like to work on and see blossoming in the new you.

Take the time to do some of those exercises to help you identify what you really want and what assets you have that will help you in this process.

	What I really want	What are my assets?
Personal Development Emotions/Thoughts		
Health		
Family/Parenting		
Relationship Intimate		
Career/Profession		
Spiritual Awareness		
Relationship Social/Fun		
Finance		
Inner Work/Self-Development		
Energy		

I would like you to look at each of these elements in detail, but it would take so much space in this book. Go to the www.renaissancewomanbook.com/theworkbook to upload files to support you in this process. It is important to identify your strengths and use them to support you even if you are struggling in some area of your life.

Creating Your Rebirth Renaissance Woman Vision

You would like to live your dream life. You have spent some time identifying what you really want. I hope you took the time to write down all of your desires, values, beliefs, strengths and weaknesses. Until now, there was always a good excuse preventing you to realize this dream. At some point, you just need to let go of the past and jump into this new possibility. What is the worst that can happen? It's time to consider new options. What would you get by living your dream?

How many times did you postpone making a difficult decision? And once you took it, what happened after that? What is the most difficult: making the choice or living the consequences of it?

There are so many questions, so let's try to focus on creating the vision of the woman you would like to be.

Preemptive Actions

Considering what you really want, identify at least three areas that you might want to see changed in order to live a better life:

- Self-Development—Emotions/Thoughts
- Health
- Family/Parenting
- Relationship Intimate
- Career/Profession
- Spiritual Awareness
- Relationship Social Relationship/Fun
- Finance
- Energy

When you are scared to start something new, there are two questions you should ask yourself:

- What would I do if I were not scared?

- What is the worst that can happen?

For each:

- Rate from one to ten how you feel you are doing. One means, "I am unhappy, I am failing..." while ten means, "I am perfectly happy, I achieved my maximum potential..." At which level would you like to be and within which time frame?
- Which habit would you like to eliminate?

- What has been preventing you from reaching your goal until today?
- What new habit would you like to put in place?
- What would be different once you use a new habit?
- List three actions you can take toward your goal.
- What is the first step in this new direction, and when can you take this first step?
- How can you be accountable for this first step? How can you be accountable for the steps that follow?

Take notes as you are going through this very demanding exercise. Take time to reflect on each step. Any action you decide to take must be achievable and measurable. Do not try to reach for the moon right away; instead, chose smaller steps that you are confident you can achieve in a limited time period. Let's use weight loss as an example: if your goal is to lose fifty pounds, focus on eating healthier, changing the type of food you eat, exercise more, etc., and take it one day at a time.

The Rules of the Game

In order to be effective, you have to keep some very important notions in mind.

The first one is the concept of **Integrity.** Integrity is complex since it's very subjective. We feel guilty when we are "out of integrity." For example, if your goal is to go back to school and get a degree in marine biology, but

your main values are "time spent with your family" and "financial stability," you might have a hard time feeling the integrity in pursuing your dream career. You have to consider the compromises, you have to accept to achieve what you want and be in agreement with those values. Take some time to identify the moments when you are not working fully toward your goal.

You want to study toward your degree, but you actually spend your afternoon enjoying a coffee with friends. Identify the reasons of those decisions and try to make a conscious choice in your actions.

Your body will be your main barometer in finding out if you are living in alignment with your values and beliefs. Your ancestral brain (limbic brain) will react to any stress either conscious or unconscious. If you are not living in accord with your principles, it will trigger response at the body level: shortness of breath, muscle tension, pressure, etc. Listen to those messages carefully since the only way to modify any behavior in a constant way is to do it in agreement with your subconscious.

Synchronicity or the Law of Attraction is also a very important concept. Some people believe in coincidence and that things "just happen." You might be more aware and notice that the energy we express actually creates synchronicities that match our current pattern. Those synchronicities always happen, but it's up to you to be aware of them. When I started to work on this book, I paid more attention around me, and sure enough, I discovered many other writers and women's networking groups. I even discovered that my son had been an editor for his school newspaper, which he had never shared with me. It was a blessing since I was looking for someone to help me reread the first draft of this book and give me initial feedback. The universe, or whatever you want to call it, bring elements to support you towards your goal, but it is your role to notice and use those elements.

In order to achieve your dream, you may also want to "Walk the talk." What I mean by "walk the talk" is that you want to be true to yourself or at least do your best in doing so. To do that, imagine that you have accomplished your goal. Set a precise date for that. Go with your intuition and don't overthink it. Write a letter to yourself starting with these words, "I am happy, proud, and grateful now that..." Whatever you write after that is what you want to accomplish. Describe what it looks like, and how you feel about it. Be as precise as possible. Sign and date the document. You will now be accountable for this set date of accomplishment.

Wish
↓
Hope
↓
Faith
↓
Confidence
↓
Knowledge

Now, read what you have just written and consider how you feel about it. Is it a wish that it will happen, a hope that you have the strength to do it, faith that you will find in you and what is required, confidence that the universe is there for you, or knowledge that at the set date this dream is achieved? If it's only a wish or a hope, spend some time considering what is still blocking you. If you have confidence, you might just need a little push to know that you are capable of doing what you want. Knowing that in *x* days, weeks, or months you will have reached your goal, nothing prevents you to walk the talk today and behave as if it already happened. If you know that in six months your book will be published, what is preventing you from feeling and being an Author today?

Clearing your clutter, what we saw earlier in this book, is essential. In order to move forward, it is essential to let go of the past. Clutter is energy. By clearing our clutter, we make room for more positive things to come into our life. Clutter is physical, but it is also emotional. It is words not spoken, emotions not released, and sadness or anger ignored or shoveled under the carpet.

Clearing your clutter means looking at your situation in the most objective way that you are capable of. It is to consider what you have been tolerating until now and decide if you want to continue doing so. It is choosing what you want to keep or to let go of. It can be leaving a relationship in which you have been unhappy for years. It can also be choosing to stay in the relationship because it has some very good parts that are important in accordance with your values, and working actively at changing the parts that you don't like—communication, resentment, sexual interaction, etc.

The Tools

You are not on your own. There are many tools that will help you in this process of creating your vision. Here are a few that have been helpful to me and to my clients. Choose your tool or your panel of tools; some of you might prefer meditation, while others will swear by exercise. There is not a solution. There is YOUR solution. As I've said earlier, I have been able to go through some major transitions without using any antidepressants. It makes more sense to me to face fear and emotions even though it can extremely be painful. That being said, I have seen many women (or men) who needed this chemical support to go through a terrible time in their lives. The pain they were experiencing was so strong that they were not able to function without pharmacological support. Whatever your choice is about medication, there are still many tools that can help instead, or in conjunction with, an antidepressant treatment.

Have you considered things like homeopathy, acupuncture, meditation, or other stress-releasing techniques? And once you have moved to a level where you feel able to function again, which tools would be appropriate to make your vision a reality?

I will not talk in detail about homeopathy[6] or acupuncture[7] since they are tools that require the help of a professional. The goal of this book is to give you tools that you can use on your own. But do not hesitate to contact me if you are looking for a practitioner in your area. I will do my best to refer you to someone.

Meditation

Meditation is an extremely powerful skill. It is a time when you pay attention to your breath, to the fact that air is entering your body and leaving your body. It is a time when you acknowledge that your body is working on its own without you putting any thoughts into that. Your heart is beating, your muscles are holding yourself up, and your digestive system is doing its job processing the food you ingested. Thoughts are going through your brain, but you let them pass by without judging them or putting any intention in them. You can be aware of everything that is inside of you and surrounding you: the sounds, the air, the wind, the smells, but you don't let it impact or influence who you are and the way you behave during that time of meditation. Meditation is a moment of peaceful energy. It is blissfulness and calmness. It is just being and nothing more.

[6] www.homeopathic.org
[7] www.nccam.nih.gov/health/acupuncture/introduction

If a few years ago someone has suggested meditation to me, I would have laughed and dismissed his or her offer. Once relegated to the realm of pseudo-science, many studies have recently shown that meditation can benefit your body, mind and spirit. Meditation helps to reduce pain[8]. Researchers speculate that those who practice meditation develop a greater ability to control unpleasant feelings by turning them down, as if using a volume button in the brain.

Meditation seems to boost the immune system, lower blood pressure, ease inflammation and reduce heart risks. It is not a cure for all, but it seems that the mindfulness offered by meditation is likely to help people alleviate the symptoms associated with those problems. At the mind level, meditation increases gray matter in area tied to compassion, emotional regulation, and self-awareness. It cultivates willpower, increasing attention, focus, stress management, self-control and boost cognitive functions and that's after only a few weeks of brief daily practice. It builds self-knowledge and increases compassion and empathy. By doing so, it strengthens the ability to respond well to relationship stress and helps develop skills in communicating emotions with others, increasing relationship satisfaction at home and at work. Overall, meditation seems to be an excellent tool to ease stress and anxiety, lower the feeling of loneliness, and improve symptoms of depression.

I was at my lowest point energetically after my husband had left. Some of the physical symptoms I experienced were usually associated with PTSD, depression, and anxiety. I had a hard time falling asleep, and if I did, I would wake in the middle of the night with my mind racing and my body drenched in cold sweat. My breathing was shallow, and my heart was racing as much as my mind. I would try almost anything to make it stop, and it was at that point that I started meditating.

---

[8] www.huffingtonpost.com/2014/05/14/meditation-mind-body-spirit_n_5291361.html

Surprisingly, sitting quietly for thirty minutes was not as difficult as I thought it was. I started by sitting for ten minutes, but I soon discovered that meditation was the only time when I would actually breathe deeply or at least normally and where my over-scattered brain would take a break from worrying. One of the things that made meditation seem overwhelming to me was that I imagined it had to be done in a certain way: sitting straight for at least thirty minutes with my eyes closed and listening to peaceful music. My apologies to the purists, but I learned that meditation could come and be powerful in many shapes and colors. I started with guided meditation. It was easier than silent meditation. There was a voice reminding me to breathe and asking me to work on a mantra or an affirmation that I had previously created for myself.

I listened to this guided meditation as many times as necessary. Usually, I was meditating in the morning, but I would also listen to my recording in my bed just before going to sleep. Most of the time I will fall asleep listening to it—the calmness of the music and of my breathing would help me relax enough to actually sleep. As I started improving, I kept my meditation practice, but now it takes a different form. It can be a "classical meditation," but it can also take place while walking in nature, listening to the wind and feeling the rhythm of my feet on the ground.

The Three-Minute Morning Routine

1 minute to be grateful: Mindfulness

1 minute to visualize: Focus

1 minute to breathe: Centering

It can be five minutes in my parked car before going to an appointment. In that case, I just search for a meditation recording online for the length of time I have in front of me and just listen with my eyes closed.

Meditation is mostly about quieting your brain and focusing on the fact that you are alive: breathing, moving and noticing sounds, smells and sensations around and within yourself. If you have never meditated, start with guided meditations and follow the instructions, focus on your breathing and relax. If your mind wanders and you find yourself thinking a variety of thoughts, don't worry. Simply bring back your thoughts to focus on your breath. You can even count each breath if it helps you stay focused.

Gratitude

Gratitude, like meditation, should be part of your daily routine. Focusing on what you have rather than what you don't have will give you a different perspective about your life.

You may not have your dream job yet, but you may have the health and the skills to look for it. Your kids may be leaving home, but they are smart enough to follow their dreams. Gratitude is a way to pay attention to everything that you have within and outside of yourself to support you. When depressed, gratitude could be simply to recognize that I was breathing that day, or I managed to smile twice that evening. It was also looking around and noticing a beautiful bird, a colorful flower, or a child playing.

At some point, a friend gave me one of the best presents ever. It was a little purple notebook, small enough to be tossed into my purse. She asked me to write three positive things that I noticed every day. She called it my *little pleasures* book. One day I wrote, "Waking up after sleeping five hours straight. Taking the train on my own without panicking. Hearing the sound of a violin while walking in the street." The next day it was, "Noticing that I am alive. Seeing my brother. Sipping coffee on a terrace." Sometimes life can feel really grim, and noticing those little pleasures and treasures is a great way to get over a rough path and realize that even if everything seems to be going against you, there are still glimpses of hope.

Today, even though I am living a great life, I wake up every morning with a three-minute routine:

- One minute to thank the universe for what I have (my health, my kids, a house, a job...).
- One minute to visualize my day if it were to go the best way I can imagine it going.
- One minute or more to breathe and if possible meditate.

This simple daily routine allows me to start every day with a smile. The gratefulness makes me be conscious of what I have, the visualization helps me to get organized in my head and have a positive perspective of the upcoming day, and the breathing centers me and allows me to be in the present.

Creating an Affirmation or a Mantra

We are very good at saying what we don't want: "I don't want to be frustrated with my boss or my spouse," "I don't want to feel guilty when I think of my relationship with my sibling," "I don't want to feel disgusted when I look at myself," etc. Knowing what you don't want is actually really easy, because that's the sentence you are repeating to yourself day after day: "I am tired in the morning," "I am angry because of him," "I look ugly." Whatever you say over and over gets integrated by your system and by your brain as true. You may know it is not the truth, but after a while, your brain registers it as so and gets used to it. At this point it becomes your truth. The concept of creating an affirmation is to repeat what you want instead of what you don't want.

"I am angry when my sibling asks me for money" becomes "I feel proud knowing that I do my best to help my sibling." "I am frustrated by the twenty pounds I have recently put on" becomes "I am confident that I have the willpower to choose a healthier lifestyle."

The first time I personally used that tool was to transform the sentence, "I can't accept the idea of my husband leaving," into, "I feel at peace knowing that I can let him go." It might be difficult to find this sentence defining what you actually want. It may even feel strange to pronounce it at first. The new sentence has to be in congruence with your values and beliefs and should be a stretch, but say something that you could imagine yourself doing if the "stars align." Once you find this new sentence or affirmation, make it as simple as possible. Then you can repeat it as a mantra and think about what you will gain from living in accordance to this new sentence.

If I know that I can feel at peace in letting my husband go, I will smile again, I will feel safe... Please try to keep those benefits as positive statements. Instead of saying, "I am not afraid of being lonely," say, "I am confident that I can be on my own." Take the time to list all the benefits you can think of and, once you are done with that, list all the sub-benefits you could get from each of your benefit. Soon enough you will find a list of positive results and feelings that you would experience once your affirmation is reality[9].

This process is very similar to **visualization.** Creating an affirmation is more about the way you would feel, while visualization tends to be more pragmatic and practical. Visualization and affirmation are beyond a dream. They are something that you aspire to. They are a way to create your future now. They are the master plan on how to create this Renaissance woman who exists within you.

---

[9] If you want some help creating an affirmation to support you in your journey email me at fab@renaissancewomanbook.com and I will be happy to help.

You have a vision of what you want. This vision needs to be as precise as possible.

You have a firm intention to make this vision a reality. An **intention** is a message you give to yourself about what you are planning to do. When you have a firm intention, you commit your energy to your goal or task.

Take Action

Now it's time to devise a plan to get you there. Look back to the beginning of this chapter at the items you want to develop or improve. For those top three items, indicate one to three actions you could take to make a change. You can do that for each area you would like to work on in your life. Identify the top three areas that you want to improve on.

They might be things that you consider assets that you want to improve upon, areas that you would like to develop within yourself, or simply things that you are interested in.

Record any thoughts, insights, or plans you have at this moment regarding those different areas.

Let's have a precise look at where you want to go. It is important to have a detailed vision. Most of the time success doesn't happen by chance. It's not enough to wander around, hoping for happiness and accomplishment. In *The Secret*, author Rhonda Byrne asks us to see what we want as if it were part of our new reality, but she never tells us to sit and wait for it to happen. The most successful and happiest people are those who have a clear picture of what they want, of where they are going, and then they take the required action to get there. Consider each aspect of your life and visualize your dream result one year from today. Take the time to state how different your life will look and give as many details as possible. Do the same thing by visualizing where you will be three years from now. Do the same thing projecting another five years. What would it look like?

The Conscious-Change Model

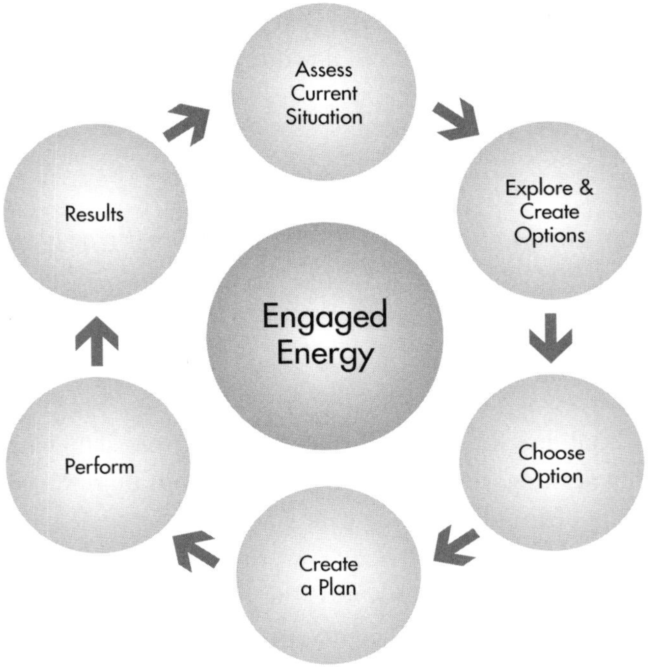

You won't be able to accomplish most of the things without a minimum of engagement.

Engagement is your willingness and ability to do something about any particular goal, task, or project you would like to accomplish or to commit to. It is the energy you will put into any role you want to take in your life. It reflects how much anabolic energy you will be able to allocate toward this goal and how you will be able to access this positive, creative, and constructive type of energy. The only way to get engaged is by actually embracing the possibility of the change. By going through the first two phases of the transition process, you let go of your past and of what you were until now. It's time to create the future you envision. Wanting to change is actually a huge part of the process of change. Your ability to accomplish a task depends on your skills, knowledge, and capability to perform this particular task. It reflects WHAT you do. Ability is essential for success but does not guaranty success by itself. How many times do you know what to do to achieve a certain goal but you don't actually take action or you quit in the middle? Your willingness to do something is related to your buy-in factor and your motivation.

"We delight in the beauty of the butterfly, but rarely admit the changes it has gone through to achieve that beauty."

- Maya Angelou

What I call "buy-in" is what you have to gain from achieving your goal versus doing nothing, and your motivation depends on how much energy you want to put behind achieving your goal.

It is WHY you do what you do. The more motivated you are to do something, the more it is in alignment with your values, beliefs, etc., and the more likely you will put in the efforts necessary to be successful. To accomplish something you need the ability, but also you need to be engaged in it. In order to increase your willingness, the engagement should be specific. You need to know what you want to do, why you want to do it, and how you are going to do it in order to design a plan.

Commit to your plan. Once you visualize your goal, it is important to commit to it. With commitment, you don't give yourself an option to turn around and run away, nor you play the game of the "what-if" game. In commitment, there is no looking back, and no energy dispersed in doubt or worries. A commitment based on "what if it doesn't work" will end up in "I should hold back, just in case." Take the time to reflect on what a commitment means to you. Now that you have designed your Renaissance Woman Plan, and have written down all the details about your goals, actions, feelings, etc., you must decide how committed you are to it. If you are not fully committed, take the time to consider what is holding you back and think about the steps that will make you fully committed.

One of my clients was struggling with commitment issues. Fear was holding her back.

Each time she was almost ready to "go for it," her little gremlin would show up and bring back doubts. We devised a mantra for her that stated, "Check with your intuition to be sure about what you want to do, but once you are decided do not look back." She knew she could rely on her intuition and that she was smart enough to not make an inconsiderate decision. Once she had dotted her i's and crossed her t's, she had to jump into the pool and swim.

Accountability can help you stick with a commitment. It is about doing what you said you would do and reporting to someone about that. There are many ways to keep you accountable. You can work with a coach, report regularly to a friend, or you can download apps that will require you to report your progress or share on your social network. You can also create a progress journal where you can review your intention and your vision regularly and write down where you are with your one-month, six-month, one-year, or three-year-and-beyond plan.

Finally, whatever goal you want to reach, you will have to put a maximum of positive or anabolic energy into your project in order to make it a success. Catabolic energy is predominately the energy of fear, running away, or fight. It is the energy that will help you to be cautious and will require you to think twice before acting. But at some point, catabolic will limit you from action. You need anabolic engaged energy to accomplish any goal, task, or project. There are four dimensions that contribute to this energy: spiritual, mental, emotional, and physical.

In order to be specific, just take the time to identify a current goal. On a scale of one to ten, how would you rate your level of engagement toward accomplishing this goal?

One being, "I don't want to do it," and ten being, "I really want to do it" and "I am ready to take any action necessary to achieve my goal."

Now let's examine the four dimensions of engaged energy.

Physical Energy

Your physical energy involves how much you are actually able to move and take action toward your goal. It is essential to accomplish any task and includes aspects as basic as sleep, nutrition, and physical ability, or as complex as your overall health level, your fitness level both in strength or endurance, the way you manage pain, and your environment at home or work. Lower physical energy is easier to identify because it is visible most of the time, but that doesn't make it easier to manage. You might be highly driven toward your goal, but if you operate on few hours of sleep, don't exercise, and keep eating junk food, you might find out that "powering through" challenges is not enough and you may feel depleted, if not sick. Think about the last time your physical ability was limited by an injury or an illness. What was your level of stress at that moment in your life, and how much were you able to accomplish?

A few years ago, I injured my back. I was not able to walk for more than few yards without pain, and I couldn't sit for more than fifteen minutes. I was in my late thirties but felt as old and limited than what I imagine a ninety-year-old could experience. My vitality, my sleep, and my mood were affected. I became snappy, sad, and overall depressed, and that affected everyone around me. I could barely go through my day and could in no way envision creating something new. This made me realize that in order to work toward my goal, I needed to be strong all around, which implies healthy eating habits, daily exercise, and a minimum of six hours of sleep.

Let's demonstrate the effect of physical stress with a very simple exercise. Take two fingers and press firmly under your lower ribs. There is a sore spot there. Once you found it, press on it and try to maintain a conversation. Now, have the same conversation without your fingers pressing under your ribs. You will notice that it is way more difficult to focus if your body is distracting you.

Physical engagement implies you to be aware of what your body is telling you and to adjust what you are doing to take care of yourself. Your physical wellbeing contributes to your performance and focus. It also impacts your emotional and mental energy.

Mental Energy

Your mental energy involves the brainpower you can access at a specific moment. It is your ability to stay focused, alert, and clear in order to make decisions, get new ideas, be creative, and use your intuition to decide what you do, why you want to do it, and how you are going to make it happen. Visualization is a great tool to help you get in the moment and gain clarity about your project. When you are stressed, it is very difficult to access this energy. You can increase your mental energy by establishing a clear action plan, limiting distractions, and asking for unambiguous feedback from friends or professionals if necessary.

Let's go back to your initial goal. What is your action plan? Please be as precise and specific as possible. How much time are you willing to dedicate to this goal? What has been distracting you until now, and what can you do to limit those distractions? Which skills do you have that could support you toward your goal? List three persons who could support you or give an unbiased constructive criticism.

Emotional Energy

Your emotional energy will obviously be different if you experience enthusiasm and inspiration instead of frustration and being overwhelmed. Any action will be easier if you are clear about what you want to accomplish, are in control of the situation, and are aware of what should be done and how it should be done. You also should be confident that you would able to respond more than react to any given situation.

A way to put your emotional energy on board is to accept your emotions, good or bad. Emotions are short-lived unless resisted to, remember? Recognizing how you feel without judging it as "bad" is a great start. You have the right to feel miserable. Sometimes life brings you a curved ball and all you can do is experiencing Level 1 (victim) and Level 2 (anger) type of energy. When you get there, recognize that it is just energy, just emotion coming up. Those emotions are challenging because they trigger uncomfortable or unpleasant sensations in your body, but they are there to tell you something about your goal, your values, etc. Acknowledge, validate, and accept them, and if they are preventing you from attaining your goal, challenge them. Clarify what the situation is about. Reframe what's going on. Is what you perceive to be the truth actually true, or is it biased because you are stressed or tired? What may look at first like a challenge may in fact be an opportunity. Confront your own interpretations. Look at other perspectives and take a deep breath. Sometimes that's all it takes.

Spiritual Energy

Spiritual energy is your sense of purpose and meaning in all you do in life. It is the energy involved in your sense of fulfillment or contribution. Purpose, vision, commitment, beliefs, faith, resiliency, and desire are all part of your spiritual energy and it has a major impact on your level of engagement. If you don't feel a purpose in what you are doing or if what you want to do is not in alignment with your values, you will have a very hard time taking action. Find a connection between your actions and your personal vision. Trust yourself in knowing that there is a reason you are doing what you are doing and that it is part of walking toward who you are as a person.

How important to you is the goal you identified earlier? How is working toward this goal supporting your purpose in life, and is it in accordance with your values, beliefs, and dreams? List the actions you are willing to take to accomplish your goal. Are those action in agreement with your sense of purpose and who you think you are or you should be as a person? How committed are you to your goal, and how can you increase your commitment?

Each dimension of energy affects the other. There is little that can be accomplished unless you have a sense of clarity and direction. There won't be any sense of focus if you are out of balance emotionally or if you feel physically drained. And being emotionally affected by grief can sabotage any of your plan, the same way a major physical illness can put any project at a standstill regardless of the amount of spiritual, mental, or emotional energy you put behind it. Your **total engaged energy** is how much anabolic energy you are putting toward a specific goal, role, or project in the entire four dimensions. If you are fully engaged toward change and your mental, physical, emotional, and spiritual capacities are at their maximum, your total engaged energy will be multiplied. This engaged energy is what drives your actions, and it is the determining factor in what type of result you can potentially produce. On top of that, no matter how aligned, bought in, and able you are, it will be very difficult to accomplish anything unless you want to. Wanting to change is the first step.

In order to reach any goal, accomplish any task, or fulfill any role, it is important to shift your energy from catabolic to anabolic as much as possible.

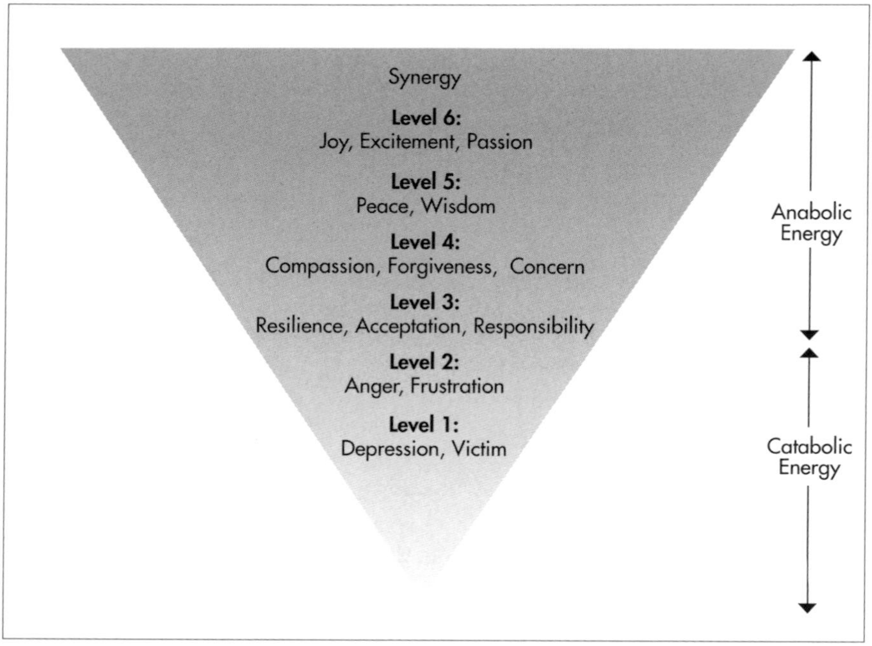

Many things can be accomplished in a forceful manner, but it is very difficult to sustainably change unless the energy you develop toward your goal is anabolic. Having a buy-in is a wonderful first step, but a buy-in without understanding and alignment of what you want to accomplish with your values and beliefs gets very challenging with time, and you might quit as soon as you encounter your first obstacle. You have to be patient and think really precisely at what you want or don't want, and that's why the limbo phase that seemed so boring was actually an essential stepping stone toward creating the future you desire.

Let's look at the way you behave at a higher level of anabolic energy. People experiencing energy at Level 5 and above aren't at the effect of the situation, nor are they finding the need to fight a situation in order to create change. The goal is not care anymore about winning or losing but more about how to create a win-win situation. In a relationship, there is no more "blame game." The two partners don't care who's at fault but more about how they can create a solution that will be agreeable to both parties. This working in harmony toward a shared goal creates a sense of peace.

At Level 6, the goal is still an ultimate target, but the pleasure is as much in reaching that goal as it is in enjoying the journey to get there. Joy and excitement to work on a project you are passionate about, having a sense of purpose, and being in alignment with your beliefs and values will get you a sense of limitless energy, creativity, and the capacity to use all your skills at their fullest, and you will be able to trust your intuition in any decision you have to make at this point.

There is an energy level above Level 6 experienced during meditation or during special times when the "stars align." Unfortunately, it is not sustainable for most people. I call it "synergy" since at that point you might use any energy, catabolic and anabolic, to work in your favor toward your goal, and there is no pressure of success because you know that whatever you will experience is what should happen. My experience with Level 6 energy and above was a beautiful moment. The expression "the sky is the limit" doesn't even make sense anymore at this point since there is actually no real limit on what we can accomplish. Any limit, whether it is physical, financial, or other, doesn't feel like an obstacle but more like part of the equation toward success.

Once I decided exactly why I was there and what was my purpose in life, I felt I had a choice over my life. My role as a spouse vanished, and I started dating other men, not because I felt I had to be with someone but because I wanted to be with someone. If that person was not the right one, I could move on from the relationship. I met wonderful men who became great friends at that time. My kids being grown up, I left my role as pure mom-caregiver and our interactions became more adult. Professionally, once I found my purpose, I became unstoppable. Within few months I started developing my coaching practice, I worked with different mentors learning new skills, I started writing, I continued sculpting, and I showed my work each time I had the opportunity. I wrote a letter to myself explaining what my life would look like one year later and surprisingly, or not, ninety-nine percent of what I wrote became reality within one year.

I became a different woman who could fully express who she was and could recognize and show her full potential. A confident woman who was working really hard at creating her dream life and was actually doing so, step by step, enjoying every single moment of this journey. I was reborn a Renaissance woman.

CHAPTER 5

Sassy, Strong, and Successful at Forty, Fifty, and Beyond

"If you don't like something, change it.
If you can't change it, change your attitude."

- Maya Angelou

The more I look at this transition called the Feminine Midlife Crisis, the more I find it difficult to see it as a crisis. I would rather consider it as a metamorphosis, a rebirth.

The first step in this path toward you as a Renaissance woman is a personal reevaluation. You cannot really change who you are unless you change your perception of life and the perception you have of yourself. This personal development is essential in order to get you to this second part of life feeling strong and proud of who you are.

The challenge was to let go of your old identity of your paradigm. It is so surprising to realize that whatever was your experience in life until now, it has impacted you and influenced the way you react to any situation you are confronted with until today. It is natural for anyone who experienced what you have would react the same way. At the same time, it is fundamental to gain consciousness. Life happens and there is nothing you can do to change it, but you can change your perspective about any situation, even the most dramatic one. Changing your perspective doesn't mean to ignore or forget, and sometimes there is no silver lining to be found. There are events, facts, or people you cannot change, and in trying to do so, you will feel miserable, you will make others around you feel miserable, and you will probably make yourself sick from the stress toxins released by your body.

A wonderful woman who I have gotten to know pretty well had to live through the terrible experience of losing two of her children. Still, I always saw her with a smile on her face and a positive attitude toward life. When I asked her how she could stay positive, her answer was that none of the tears she cried would get her kids back and that since she was living this life, the only choice she had was to make it as happy as possible.

We were born with the freedom of choice, and choosing positive emotions and behavior that supports you mentally, emotionally, spiritually, but also physically. Playfulness, gratitude, love, curiosity, serenity, and connection to others broaden our perspective and opens our minds. It simply brings back joy in our life. Negative emotions (Level 1 and 2-type of energy) are not the enemy; they are here for a reason—to keep us safe and to allow us to react in a crisis situation. You might need them to fight back or to run away from a particular situation, but brooding about the loss won't help. Once you move your energy to a more anabolic type, you will be able to observe many positive effects at your body and mental level.

Positive emotions benefit individuals with cardiovascular diseases, lower high blood pressure, and reduce the risk of diabetes. They allow us to sleep better and reduce the amount of colds, headaches, and pain, which leads to better physical fitness and increased flexibility. A positive attitude helps a person to overcome negative emotions faster and be more able to cope with a difficult situation. When you get into a happy space, more possibilities present themselves, and you access new ideas and your creativity increases.

There are so many ways to increase your positivity and your anabolic energy overall. There is no magical recipe. You just need to find yours. Here are a few suggestions.

Improve Your Mental Energy

Acknowledge and Validate Your Feelings

The absolute first step in order to become a Renaissance woman is the simplest and the most challenging at the same time. You cannot build a castle on quicksand. I cannot build a new tall, strong, and powerful lady out of clay unless I get a strong structure inside. You cannot be a strong Renaissance woman unless you find your inner power, your sense of worth, and your self-love. Everything you have experienced and lived until now makes you who you are. You have been struggling; it made you stronger. You took a wrong turn; it allowed you to pay more attention to when you have a choice. You were in a bad relationship; at least you know what you don't want anymore. You worked for years in a job you didn't like; you developed skills that will help you in any job you chose later on.

I was a biochemist. There are many skills from that time that I still use in my sculpture. I had to learn anatomy and how the human body works. I love experimenting with chemical products, and I developed many new colors for the patina of my sculptures. I worked for a few years in marketing. Obviously, this is a tool I use every day as an entrepreneur to promote my business. My marriage ended. I learned that I could live on my own and take care of myself without the help of anyone. Now I choose a partner I want to live with out of choice and not out of fear.

Life is not about punishing yourself for what you should have done differently. It is about living day after day to the best of your ability, learning from your errors, and making a better choice the next time. Challenges are what pushes us to go above and beyond. Accept when you are vulnerable. Hiding who you are by pretending to be strong or having it all figured out is actually a sign of weakness. Failing is not the problem. Everybody fails at one point or another. The difference between you and another person is how much time you will stay on the ground crying about yourself. Dry your tears, step up, and take your life back in your hands. What do you want next? What kind of woman do you want to be? What kind of woman do you want to be if you can be at your very best? Even if it's not today, even if it takes years to take the first step toward becoming who you really want to be, there will be a point in time when you will decide this first step and this will be your point of rebirth.

Visualize

Get clarity and replace the fear of the unknown with a sense of desire for what's to come. Sometimes you need to experience what you don't want in order to decide to do something about it and create what you want. Write down your goals, your aspirations, your dreams, and the steps that will get you. Describe how you will feel once you have accomplished your goal. If you are the more creative type, design a dream board. Find images of what you dream of and fill up your canvas with all your projects. Hang the board somewhere so you can look at it day after day. Create an affirmation. Find every single benefit you will get from reaching your dream. Repeat this affirmation day after day as part of a daily meditation.

Most leaders of today use visualization as part of their routine. It is way more than dreaming. It is a way to plan your goals and to set up your priorities.

Improve Your Spiritual Energy

Spirituality is a major part of the Renaissance woman's life. Spirituality is a connection with your inside world and a connection with the outside world beyond religion, even though religion can be part of it. It is recognizing your values and your beliefs and living in harmony with them as much as possible. Spirituality is learning to enjoy the present moment. We spend so much time in the past thinking of what we did, what we feel has been done to us, or what should have been. Our past is just a story, one that we cannot change. It is our choice to let it define who we are in the present or to keep it as a story that taught us valuable lessons and nothing more.

Many times when we are not dwelling on the past, we tend to project ourselves into the future and worry. What should I do? What will happen next? We start feeling like rats running in a maze without any way out. Our brain and our thoughts become the masters of our destiny.

Sometimes it is important to do nothing, to stop and realize that the life we are living is in the present. As I described earlier, one of the best way to calm down our brain is through **meditation**. Establishing a meditation routine will give you those instance of just being in the present and will help you regenerate your energy as much as a good night's sleep.

Respect Your Intuition

When you are in doubt, don't forget to check with yourself. We often tend to look to outsiders for advice and we tend to ignore our inner voice. Your inner voice has some very important things to say. You are usually the one who knows what is best for you. Listen to your body. Your sensations are the expression of your feelings and the voice of your subconscious brain. We talk about "gut feelings" for a reason: headaches, stomachaches, shoulder or neck tensions—pains of any kind are usually a way to let you know that you are not in alignment with your values.

Celebrate What You Have Accomplished so Far

The pursuit of passion and happiness is like a treasure hunt. The path is never clearly laid out, but we get clues along the way that give us assurance

that we're not out of our minds for pursuing our dreams. Celebrate each step and what you learned along the way, and use it as a reminder to not give up when the end result isn't happening as quickly as you may want it to. Use kind words to talk to yourself. Be patient with yourself. Renaissance is not a race. Renaissance is walking an unknown path with an open mind and a positive spirit. Each step is a victory on its own. Don't compare yourself to others. Everyone has his or her own journey. Just pay attention to what you want, enjoy the ride, enjoy every little progress, and be sure that everything will happen exactly the way it is supposed to happen.

You are Fabulous

You have everything you need within you to accomplish what your heart desires. Don't let fear stop you. When in doubt, I always ask myself, "What will I do when I'm not afraid?" What would you do if you weren't scared of failing, of lacking money, energy, support, or whatever else? What would you do if you were going into the world knowing that you can build a masterpiece out of this pack of clay called life? Your life is your masterpiece. Make it what you want. Make it as colorful, shiny, and glittery as you want.

In a recent speech[10], Jim Carrey told students about his father who chose to become an accountant instead of becoming a comedian because he was afraid he would not be able to make a consistent income as an artist. His father was eventually laid off from a job that he didn't even like and struggled after that. You can also fail at what you don't want. Find a balance and fight for what you want and not something you feel you have to do to be safe. As far as we know, we have one life. This is your life. Enjoy every moment and make it as fabulous as you are.

"Shoot for the moon. Even if you miss, you'll land among the stars."

- Brian Littrell

[10] www.youtube.com/watch?v=q2rVDCrt6QY

Improve Your Emotional Energy

Smile

Smile when you are happy, but also smile as much as possible when you feel sad. Smile to others but also smile at yourself. Studies have shown that smiling at yourself in the mirror will increase your positivity[11]. It may feel silly to look at your reflection in a mirror and smile when you feel miserable, but it works. Maybe not on the first day, maybe not in the second. It usually takes twenty-one days to change a habit.

I once promised myself to look into my eyes every morning in the mirror and always stay proud of that person I would see every day. I kept this promise during the difficult times, and every single morning I spent a few seconds looking at my reflection, telling myself that I would be okay and smiling. Some days it was a sad smile, some days it was a hopeful one, but I kept on smiling, and day after day I saw my reflection smiling back at me, and it made me happy for one minute or for the rest of the day. It is a very easy thing to do. Just try for a week and see how it impacts you.

Take the Time to Realize How Beautiful You Are

Since you are in front of the mirror, look at yourself once more and notice everything you like in what you see. We have this unfortunate tendency to focus on what we don't like. Just make a conscious decision to look and enjoy what you actually do like. "I like the shadow of my left shoulder." "I like the color of my eyes..." I am sure you will find something. The more you focus on what you like, the less you will focus on what you don't like. Be

[11] Happiness: The Science Behind Your Smile - By Daniel Nettle

kind to yourself. You are not perfect. Who is? You are as perfect as you can be at this moment in time. Perfection comes with vulnerability, with the capacity to discover that you can love yourself the way you are. It doesn't mean letting you go. On the contrary, once you start loving YOU, you will take care of you. You will cherish those beautiful details and work on the ones you would like to change.

Humor Always Works

Learn to laugh with others and learn to laugh on your own. A great way to improve your emotional energy is to laugh. A study[12] states that the average four-year-old laughs three hundred times a day, and a forty-year-old laughs less than twenty times a day. Still, laughter enlivens us. It reduces the level of stress hormones like cortisol and dopamine. It increases the level of endorphins and infection-fighting antibodies. It increases resistance to diseases and improves blood flow. And, of course, it improves our mood. When we laugh, we are more hopeful and engaged. We are friendlier and perceived to be more attractive and radiant. Increase your laugh quota by surrounding yourself with friends, family, and people that you love. Laugh is contagious. If others around you laugh, it will tend to trigger you to laugh as well.

Be Vulnerable and Surround Yourself with Loved Ones

Don't lose your time crying about your fate, but be brave enough to accept your emotions for what they are—a way to express your thoughts and your feelings. Strong women tend to do everything on their own, and when things are getting difficult, they push their problems under a carpet to ignore them. Issues might resolve themselves on their own

[12] Do Children Laugh Much More Often Than Adult Do? By Rod A. Martin

but not always, and pretending that everything is going perfectly well when it's not doesn't help. It is okay to not be at your top. Accept that you cannot always make it on your own and to reach for help when you need it.

Sometimes we don't want to ask for help. We are afraid to become a "burden" to the people who love us. You would be happy to be there for a friend or family member reaching out for help. You would feel like you have accomplished something positive and meaningful. Why deprive those who love you from the pleasure of helping you? People who love you will enjoy being by your side in your journey. Don't be afraid to reach out.

Reach out for Professional Help

I always repeat to my kids, "If you don't know what to do or how to do it, ask someone who knows for help." Still, it took me some time to reach out for support. I wanted to make it on my own. Part of making it on your own is recognizing when too much is too much. Sometimes you just need someone by your side. A coach, a therapist, or a spiritual leader can give the little push that will make you take the first step and the following ones. He or she will be there when you have doubts or to cheer you on along the way. He or she can be your emotional support and will help you gain clarity on what you really want to achieve.

Sometimes help is around the corner and is available for free. In the south San Francisco Bay Area where I live, there is this wonderful house called Deborah's Palm[13] where you can go anytime you're in need for support, whether it is someone to talk to, a warm meal, a sweet smile, financial advice, or professional help. Ask around in your community to find out if there is a similar organization.

---

13 Deborah's Palm - www.deborahspalm.com

Improve Your Physical Energy

Respect Your Body

It is essential to take care of your body and be in the best health possible in order to reach any goal, take any role, or accomplish any task. As women in our forties and fifties, our faces and bodies start feeling the impact of the years. It is natural. Obviously, every woman experiences her midlife years differently. A mix of menopause and aging, as well as midlife stresses typically cause most of the changes occur during this period. Estrogens and progesterone level decline way before menopause, affecting women's mood as early as their late thirties. Most women experience natural menopause between the ages of forty and fifty-eight, with the average being at age fifty-one. No matter what your age is, a healthy lifestyle is essential for good physical energy, but this is even more the case when you arrive at your midlife because of the hormonal changes associated with pre-menopause and menopause.

Some of the main components affecting your mood and your physical energy are your diet, your sleep habits, and your physical activity.

Eat a Balanced Diet

The US Dietary guidelines[14] recommend that we eat a balanced diet from all the food groups but also that we reduce fat, saturated fat, cholesterol, sodium, and sugar in the foods that we eat. There are many diets to lose weight, gain weight, or to get a healthy lifestyle. Whatever your choice is, keep in mind that balance and moderation is the secret toward a healthy body. Doctor Gurle[15] suggests that you never go for a second helping: "Your body knows what it needs. If you have filled up your plate once, you should not fill it another time. Your brain calibrated what it needed the first time." If you are overweight, the best way to lose body fat is to eat fewer calories and to participate in aerobic exercises. An excess of one hundred calories a day

[14] www.health.gov/dietaryguidelines/2015.asp
[15] www.totalcarepractice.com

can cause a ten-pound gain in a year, and those one hundred extra calories could be burned up by a twenty- to thirty-minute daily walk.

A Weight Watcher representative explained to me, "Awareness and conscious choice are a major part of weight control. Reduce portion sizes and choose less calorie-dense foods for example. If you tend to respond to emotional challenges with food, a goal could be to replace a food solution with a non-food-based solution. It is okay to take baby steps. In a period of stress, you might have to go from grabbing the bag of potato chips to choosing a bag of carrots instead, but ultimately trying to find something that doesn't involve food is the most helpful. Trying to figure out the root emotional feeling you are in need of is the key. This could be calling a friend when you are bored or lonely, or going on a walk when you are anxious."

Exercise Regularly

It is frequent to observe a decrease in strength and flexibility during the midlife. Many people think that we tend to slow down with age and do less. For the most part, this is not true. Physical decline is not an inevitable consequence of aging, and crying over it will not make you feel younger. As we advance in age, it is extremely important to keep physically active. Much of the physical limitation attributed to aging is in fact the consequence of inactivity, disease, or poor nutrition.

The good news is that improving your lifestyle and exercising can help. Physical activity provides protection against coronary heart disease but also against other chronic diseases such as diabetes, arthritis, hypertension,

certain cancers, and osteoporosis. Overall, regular exercise will help you stay in good shape, but it will also improve your mood. It will ease tension and reduce the amount of stress you feel. Doctor Gurle suggests that you include weight training as part of your exercise routine to compensate for the muscle loss linked to aging. On top of looking better and feeling stronger, muscles burn more calories than fat.

As I was going through my own struggles, I increased my level of exercise to ninety minutes a day. I was not crying during that active time. My brain was focusing on moving my body instead on focusing on whatever was causing me stress. I was releasing every single ounce of tension by moving my energy.

It was not always easy, and there were some days when I didn't want to move from my couch, but I did it every day. After a while, it became part of my routine. First thing in the morning before heading to work, I exercise, and sometimes when I was feeling lonely and sad in the evenings, I would go back to the gym. It kept my mind and my body busy in a healthy way.

Choose something that you like. Whether it's walking, running, biking, swimming, dancing, weight lifting, yoga, Pilates, or other. What it is doesn't have so much importance as long as you're moving. I like running or walking because it is an outdoor activity, and because the rhythm of my feet on the ground gives me a sense of peace. I love dancing because it's fun. Yoga and Pilates keeps my back and my flexibility in check. But it is my routine. It is important that you find yours and, once you do, put it in your schedule. You deserve to take care of yourself. Too often women exercise after they've finished everything else that they had to do or have taken care of everybody around them. It is your time. It's your moment to be healthy and in good spirit, and you are your priority. Mark your calendar. Make an appointment with yourself, and once it's there stick to it. This appointment with your body is as important as an appointment with a client. If you don't respect that, your body might remind you by forcing you to schedule an appointment with a doctor.

One more benefit of exercise is to improve sleep. As we grow older, sleep patterns and sleep needs might change. A peaceful sleep and rest are essential rejuvenators. Be sure to include rest periods in your daily exercise program but also try to get enough sleep every day.

Improve Your Personal Relationships

Midlife is the time when many women evaluate their relationship. I won't be talking about women living in abusive or extreme situations but about those who have married and started raising a family in their late twenties and early thirties. I'm speaking about those who have reached this point after ten, fifteen, or twenty years when their kids grow up, their parents get old, and they are reconsidering what they want for the next forty-plus years of their life.

A friend once told me, "Women get married hoping their husband will change, but he will stay the same while men get married hoping their wife will never change and she does." Obviously, it is a cliché, but the person you are today in your midlife is definitely not the girl your spouse married years ago. When you know what you want or don't want any more in your life, you compromise less, and if your spouse is not on board, you have very few options: you stay or you go.

There are many ways to leave a relationship. The most obvious one is to open the door and leave, but in many cases, leaving is simply checking out. I had the opportunity to talk to many men about their marriage. They often told me the same thing: "She is not here anymore," "She is not interested by sex anymore," "I feel like I am part of the furniture." It might only be a perception, but there is some truth in what they are experiencing. Women in transition tend to pay less attention to their partner. They are busy trying to reconnect with themselves. They are challenged by their aging appearance. They reconsider their career, their role, and their purpose. At the same time, men are facing their own challenge.

And unless the couple communicates clearly about what is going on, one of them or both might call it quits and leave the relationship one way or another.

Twenty percent of women between the age of forty-five and fifty-five are divorced (U.S. Census divorce data 2012[16]) and in 2010, one in four divorces affects people fifty and older. Women are living longer, healthier, and are more financially independent than ever. They want to get more out of life and are open to end a marriage that no longer works for them. Rather than feeling stuck, they realize that they can live out a few more decades without feeling trapped in a dysfunctional relationship. It might be a painful reaction to a temporary problem related to their own transition, or the best decision that will allow them to approach this second part of life in a different way.

Being Single

Being single after forty-five is an interesting situation. Hopefully, if you enter the world of single, you will have spent some time to know what you want and what you don't want out of a relationship. The secret to finding true love is that there is no secret. Hopefully, you are wiser, stronger than in your twenties, and share your truer self with the world out there. My personal experience with dating at forty-five is that I'm a better version of myself. I know more about who I am, what I want, and what and who inspires me or not. I still feel young enough and I know that I am as beautiful outside and inside. Most men who I talked to shared that women in their forties and fifties tend to be more self-confident, and even though their body might not be as perfect as a twenty-year-old or their face show few wrinkles, self-assurance and self-love make them very attractive. At any age and in any relationship, knowing what you want, who you are, being authentic, and loving yourself is the key to success.

"Life doesn't happen to you. It happens for you."

- *Jim Carrey*

[16] www.washingtonpost.com/blogs/wonkblog/wp/2014/03/27/divorce-is-actually-on-the-rise-and-its-the-baby-boomers-fault/
www.census.gov/hhes/socdemo/marriage/data/cps/index.html

I'm not saying it is easy. You have probably heard dating horror stories, and of course some of them are true. When I became single after a twenty-year marriage, I was vulnerable and was not sure about what my experience of dating would be after so many years. You will get from the dating scene what you put into it. If you approach the situation with fear and apprehension, men who will confirm what you think about life will probably approach you. Instead of focusing on what you don't want, spend some time thinking about what you do want in a new relationship. You might not find the love of your life right away, but you will have a lot of fun in the process.

Realize that life doesn't happen TO you but FOR you. You will meet incredible men and women you might connect with at different levels. Most of them will simply become friends. Some might even become fierce enemies and teach you what you don't want out of a relationship. You attract the person who is the best for you at any specific moment. This person might be valuable as a learning experience. He or she might be someone who will share your life for few hours, days, or months. Don't judge yourself. Do your best and stay clear about who you are. Recognize your value. You will attract the person you think you deserve. If you think you deserve the best, you will attract the best. Do not forget, you don't need anyone to make you happy. Happiness is within you. The only person you will live with for the rest of your life is yourself. So start by loving yourself and you will find the right man or woman to love you if it's what you want.

Being in a Relationship

Statistics shows that many marriages end up in divorce, but fortunately there are still a lot of couples who decide to stay together. Relationships change with time. It is extremely important to share your experience about midlife with your partner. You might not experience the same type of relationship you used to have at the beginning of your marriage, but you could experience something even richer. The first ten or twenty years of your marriage was probably about building a family. Now your kids are getting older. They might already have left for college or to their own life.

If it's not the case yet, they require less of you, and you know that you will become an "empty nester" soon enough. What will be your purpose as a couple after that? If you are not Dad, Mom, and children, who will you be? It is important to redefine your new identity as a person but also as a couple. One of my friend once declared, "I am the ultimate empty nester: my kids left for college and my wife decided to finish the master's degree she always dreamed of." The line was very thin from this statement to growing apart. It was important for them to reconnect with who they were independently, but in order to save their marriage it became equally important to determine what they wanted to do together. A lot of self-work and couple-work was necessary, but they managed to stay independent and together at the same time.

Whether you have been in a relationship for many years or you are starting a new relationship, there are few essential things to keep in mind:

You cannot change the other person. Nobody has the power to change your partner besides him/herself. You can express your feelings about a situation, you can share behavior that you like or don't like, but don't ask the person you love to change. He/she might do it out of love for you, but it won't be sustainable unless he/she is the one who wants the change. Since you cannot change your partner, maybe you should start changing your own perception of the situation.

- If you feel like a victim and behave like one, there is a good chance that your partner will confirm that for you. In a relationship, your partner is your best mirror and the person we love the most will make us react the most.

- If we blame the other and they blame us, the situation will end up in an argument. The only way to get out of

> In a relationship, sometimes being right is not the most important thing.
>
> Do you want to be right or be happy?

a relationship "victim-abuser" or "aggressor-aggressor" is if one of the partners in the relationship steps out of the cycle and starts to look for a solution. You can only hope that the other will follow your lead. You only have full power over your own behavior and reaction. Be brave and become the first one to find the silver lining. Put yourself in your partner's shoes. Winning an argument may feel great in the short term, but what is the most important—being right or being happy with the person you love?

- Know who you are and love yourself. Choose a partner and stay with your partner because you love him/her, but don't become codependent. I spent many years trying to be the person I thought my husband wanted me to be. Once he left, I decided I was tired of trying and I chose to become myself. After our divorce, my ex gave me the biggest compliment I ever heard: "You became the woman I knew you could be." Your partner is hopefully with you because he/she loves you. He/she wants to be with you because you are you, not because you try to be someone else. Be authentic. You will enjoy yourself more and you might be surprised to discover that it is exactly what he/she wants from you.

Renaissance women are loving women, but they are not dependent on their partner for their well-being. They are with who they are out of choice not out of fear. They know they can live by themselves. They have great, purposeful and fulfilling lives, and they don't need anyone to make them feel complete. But sharing this life with someone is the icing on the cake they might choose if they want to.

> Be with someone because you want to not because you need to.

Your Sexual Life

There is no real evidence that women's sexual desire decreases in the midlife. In fact, one of the largest surveys of women and their sexual desire found very similar rates of low sexual desire among premenopausal and postmenopausal women[17]. It is still important to acknowledge the fact that changes in hormone levels can have an impact on a woman's sexual desire and pleasure. If you experience some physical changes or pains, don't hesitate to consult a physician. But the most important component that will make your sexual relationship satisfying is not hormonal but emotional. Midlife is a time of change, and if you feel unhappy with your life there is a good chance that your sexuality is not at its top. Being happy of who you are, being proud of what you are accomplishing, and feeling desirable will increase your attractiveness and your libido.

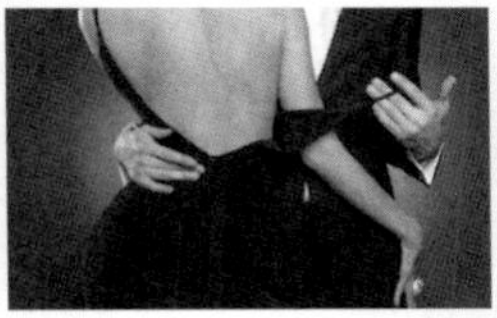

Be Successful

Follow Your Professional Dream

Along the life at home and its challenge, women face more and more challenge at work. Women who decided not to work to raise their children might find themselves with a major reevaluation of their life once their children leave home. Some women pursue their role as "helicopter moms," watching their children's every move who have now become adults. Fortunately, women often go back to the workforce if they didn't work, or increase their professional workload if they already had a job. It is important for anybody to find a purpose, a sense of belonging and direction. This can be achieved by following your professional dream.

"Let yourself be silently drawn by the stronger pull of what your really love."

- Rumi

[17] www.menopause.org/for-women/sexual-health-menopause-online

Most of the time, we work to get an income, but something women long for is a blissful career. This doesn't always mean a job that brings a lot of money, but a job that they would be willing to do for free if they didn't have to pay the bills. They want a calling, something they do knowing that is what they were meant to do.

In order to get a blissful career you need to know that you're using your full potential. Whether your skills are focused on creativity, working with people, using tools, or researching information, it is essential that you recognize your talents in order to use them. The next step is to apply those skills to something that you are passionate about. Ask yourself if the job you are considering is something you will still enjoy in ten years. Once you have identified your potential and passion, work hard and smart so what you offer is unique and valued. Since you are doing something that you are passionate about, there is a good chance you won't mind the extra hours.

Whatever job you choose, it will become one of the facets of the diamond of your life. Take the time to choose carefully. You may have to compromise, but pay attention to your values. If your main value is spending time with your friends and family, choosing a time-consuming job might not be the best idea. If you enjoy connection with others, don't take a job where you will be isolated behind your computer. You need the income, but take the time to reflect on what kind of job you really want to spend your days with. It is usually possible to make a good income doing something you like, or you might want to tweak your job description to make it correspond more to your aspirations.

Becoming an Entrepreneur

A lot of Renaissance women chose to become entrepreneurs. It is a great way to create balance in life and fulfill your purpose. Entrepreneurship attracts many women dissatisfied with corporate America but most women make this choice to build something they consider valuable and in alignment with their purpose in life. They have more flexibility, often a better income, and a potentially more meaningful work. They build businesses that usually match their spirit, values, and needs. Of course, they work very hard, but they use their potential doing something they are passionate about and this is often the recipe for success. In the *Harvard Business Review Blog Network*, Tony Schartz says, "An effective modern leader requires a blend of intellectual qualities—the ability to think analytically, strategically and creatively—and emotional ones, including self-awareness, empathy and humility... I meet far more women with this blend of qualities than I do men."

Live Successfully

There are many definitions for success; money is only one of them. As an artist, an author, and a coach, being successful is not always measured by how much I have in my bank account every month. Like everyone, I need to have a roof over my head and food on the table. Beyond that, success is one of my sculpture pieces being juried in a museum. It is someone looking at it and being touched by what I was trying to express. Success is working with a client who is going through a difficult time and seeing a huge smile on her face after a session. Success is someone reading this book and deciding to walk on the path toward finding whom they are.

What is your definition of success at work? At home? How do you want to be remembered by others? What do you want them to say about you? And, most importantly, what do you want to experience and feel that will let you know that you are successful in your own terms?

Be Financially Smart

The input I got from Mehran, a financial expert from Comerica Bank, made so much sense. You should never put yourself into credit card debt to go shopping. At the beginning of the month, take care of what you have to pay and create a budget. If you have something left for fun after that, then go ahead. If you have some saving in a 401K or an IRA, try to never use them to pay out your debt. Get the help from a professional to help you if necessary, and don't forget to "pay yourself first" then take care of others.

Beautiful Inside Out but Also Outside In

Being a Renaissance Woman, you are proud of who you are and of what you achieved. Beauty comes from within, but it can also be shown outside too. When I sculpt clay to create a "sassy lady," I spend some time working on an inside structure called "armature" that will support the piece, then I shape each line and volume around it. I enhance a shape or a shadow to express a feeling, an attitude, or an emotion. But once I am done creating the gesture I don't want to stop there. I polish the outside of my piece, rework a line, I smooth out an area, and I don't stop until my sculpture expresses what I want but also looks the way I want.

Feeling 5: La charmeuse by Fabienne Slama Bismuth

It is the same thing in life. You spend time working on your goal and achieving your dream. You become the professional you want to be. You have a great relationship. You have a sense of purpose and direction and this is fantastic. You should also spend some time on looking good. It is a way to celebrate your femininity. It is a way to love yourself and honor who you are: a Renaissance woman, a woman—**YOU**.

Take Care of Your Skin and Hair

With age, skin loses its elasticity because of hormonal changes. As a result, lines and wrinkles begin to appear. At the same time, hair gets grayer and thinner. There is nothing you can do to reverse time, but you can start dyeing or changing your hairstyle to accommodate these changes and enhance your attributes.

As a woman in her midlife, it is important to take care of your look and especially of what the universe has given you—a body.

I had the privilege to talk to many professionals in the beauty industry. Their advice is to take care of your skin as a young woman and continue on for the rest of your life.

If you just started to do it in your fifties, don't panic if you start to see those first wrinkles.

Establishing a routine of taking care of your skin for five to ten minutes every day will not reverse time but it will help repair some of the damage caused by the years and enhance your natural beauty.

Suggestions from a Hairstylist

Hairstyles designed to flatter the face of a midlife woman can be as attractive and trendy as any style. Go to a reliable hairstylist. Going to a hair salon and take care of yourself in a way that translates your inner beauty and shows it outside. Rocio from Juut Salon explained, "There is no perfect style for women over 40. Choose what makes you feel beautiful. If money is an issue, your hairstylist can usually accommodate your needs but don't compromise on the quality of the work. You are worth it." She shared to me that women walk taller leaving the salon than when they came in. It's obviously because they feel more beautiful, but maybe because someone was paying full attention to them and their well-being during that time.

Suggestions from Fashion Experts

Clothing for middle-aged women doesn't have to be frumpy or even age appropriate. It all boils down to finding the balance between flattering and trendy. Women of all ages want to feel pretty and feminine in an outfit that looks pulled together, sexy, and professional. Above all, it has to flatter your body and reflect your personality and sense of style. Usually less is more, and a well-tailored piece will do way better for you than something that screams, "Look at me!" Go for simple and accessorize with jewelry or a fun accent piece like a scarf. Play up your best feature. With age comes wisdom, and by now you should have a good idea what cuts or colors work best for you. Try on different styles at the store, but choose what makes you feel good about your figure more than that outfit that you liked in a photo in a latest fashion magazine.

I always spend money on underwear. As a French woman, I love beautiful lingerie. No one will probably notice what you are wearing under your clothes, but you will know, and it will contribute to you feeling special about yourself. And good-fitting, comfortable, and well-adjusted lingerie will enhance your attributes in a way that will be showing up even under your clothes.

You are a beautiful, strong, and sexy woman. Allow what you are showing up on the outside to represent that inside beauty that you have taken the time to develop. Wear makeup and accessorize your clothing. It doesn't have to be over the top, but more of a way to express the fact that you are proud to be who you are as a woman.

EPILOGUE

Heroine Journey

Welcome to your new you.

Welcome to this woman you knew you could be.

Welcome to your dream.

Welcome to your new life.

Congratulation for going through your Heroine Journey.

It was not easy to get there. You had to experience tears, pain, frustration, and anger. You had to fight your own demons, the regrets from your past, and the anxiety about your future.

Today, here you are: the beautiful you, the strong you, the vulnerable you, a woman with her power and her vulnerability. Your journey doesn't stop here. Life will come to you with its ups and downs. Enjoy every step of your new path. The goal is important, but the journey itself is what life is about, and you are ready to experience it fully.

Whether you decide to focus on your family, your relationship, or your career, you know that you can dream and dream big, and you can appreciate your life and be grateful for what you have while trying to achieve even more.

You are a Renaissance Woman after all. A caterpillar who metamorphosed herself and managed to emerge unarmed and more beautiful than ever from its cocoon. A woman who realizes that she is just perfect the way she is today. A woman who enjoys her present and thrives for what she will be able to accomplish in her future.

Welcome, gorgeous. Whoever you are, whatever words you can use to define yourself. Vulnerable, strong, sassy, sexy, sensuous, successful, powerful, sensitive, caring, loving... Welcome to this world, welcome to your world.

Today, you are at peace. You are peace. You are you.

Scan the QR Code or visit my Facebook page.
www.facebook.com/renaissancewomanbook
Like my page and look out for new posts and updates!

ACKNOWLEDGEMENTS

There are so many people I would like to thank for helping me in the creation of this book. First, I would like to recognize the great work and dedication from Black Card Books™ and my publishing team. This book could never have come to life if it were not for your help, support, and the occasional kick in the rear end.

Thank you to my friend Maggy who helped me develop the content of this book and was my sounding board during many phone conversations between California and New York.

I am eternally grateful for my mentors and coaches who first helped me get through my own Renaissance Journey and later on became my teachers, allowing me to pass on this knowledge to you. Thank you, Randy Hold, you are my savior. I would not be standing here today if it were not for your help. Keith Miller, your coaching skills will always challenge me in the best way. Linda, I am always grateful for our eye-opening weekly conversation.

Thanks to iPEC for becoming the coaching institute I first trained with.

Thank you to my son Alex for supporting me in this project and being patient with me when I couldn't focus on him as much as I should have. Thank you for being my editor, critic, and best supporter.

Thanks for those who spent the time to read my drafts and gave all the constructive criticism I needed. This includes my always friends Markus and Alain.

It might be surprising to some of you, but I would like to acknowledge my ex-husband who, by leaving me, gave me back the best present ever: The power to know who I am as an independent woman. I know that he will be proud of my accomplishments even though he is not part of my life anymore.

Last but not least, I would like to thank my friends and clients who served as inspiration for many stories illustrating my message. Working with each of you has made me realize how much I love what I do, and I am thankful for how much I learn from each of your journeys. You are wonderful.

Gitane
freedom of style
www.gitanestyle.com
Clothing for the free-spirited woman
A multi-faceted living space more than just a store that sells clothes. We are passionate about the service we give to our customers. At Gitane, we want everyone walking through the door to relax, enjoy one another's company and to walk out feeling inspired and looking great.
Downtown Menlo Park
855 Santa Cruz Ave.
Menlo Park, CA 94025
Downtown Los Altos
334 State St.
Los Altos, CA 94022

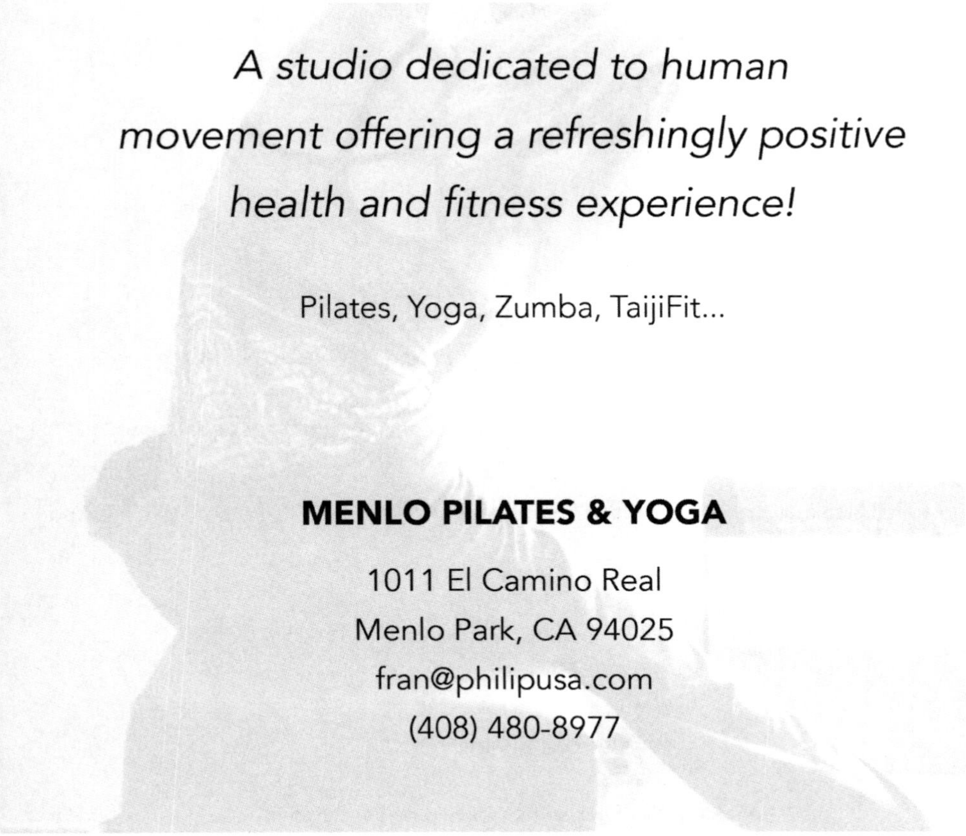

OTHER BOOKS RECOMMENDED BY BLACK CARD BOOKS™

The Millionaire Mindset
How Ordinary People Can Create Extraordinary Income
Gerry Robert

ISBN: 978-1-927411-00-1

CHAOS
How Business Leaders Can Master the Power of Focus
James M. Burgess

ISBN: 978-3-161484-10-0

Messy Manager
Double Your Sales and Triple Your Profits
Jean-Guy Francoeur

ISBN: 978-0-9786-663-0-9

The ACE Model
Winning Formula for Audit Committees
Sindi Zilwa

ISBN: 978-1-927892-24-4

Mealtimes Without Mayhem
The Easy to Follow, How to Guidebook to Get Your Family to Eat Together
Jo Turner

ISBN: 978-1-927411-04-9

Creative Culture
The Heart and Soul of South Africa
Bathandwa Mcuba

ISBN: 978-1-927411-65-0

Is This It?
How Successful People Get More Life Out of Life
Adam Fitzpatrick

ISBN: 978-1-927411-02-5

TIME IS UP!
How to Stop Procrastination and Start Achieving Your Goals
Berns David Lucanas

ISBN: 978-1-927892-47-3